Wa ght

THE S FOX

a selection of the writings
of George Fox and early Friends
with introductions by
John Lampen

QHS

QUAKER HOME SERVICE · LONDON

First published April 1981
ISBN 0 85245 155 5

Quaker Home Service
Friends House, Euston Road, London NW1 2BJ

*Cover designed by John Blamires on
an idea by John Lampen*

---

*Printed in Great Britain in 11/12 Photon Times by
Headley Brothers Ltd., 109 Kingsway, London WC2B 6PX,
and Ashford, Kent TN24 8HH.*

Contents

For a short time, ordinary people were freer from the authority of church and social superiors than they had ever been before, or were for a long time to be again. By great good fortune we have a pretty full record of what they discussed. They speculated about the end of the world and the coming of the millenium; about the justice of God in condemning the mass of mankind to eternal torment for a sin which (if anyone) Adam had committed; some of them became sceptical about the existence of hell. They contemplated the possibility that God might intend to save everybody, that something of God might be within each one of us. They founded new sects to express these ideas. Some considered the possibility that there might be no Creator God, only nature. They attacked the monopolization of knowledge within the privileged professions, divinity, law, medicine. They criticised the existing education structure, especially the universities, and proposed a vast expansion of educational opportunities. They discussed the relation of the sexes and questioned parts of the protestant ethic. The eloquence, the power, of the simple artisans who took part in these discussions is staggering. Some of it comes across in print—Fox the shepherd, Bunyan the tinker, Naylor the yeoman.[1]

Christopher Hill

Of all Christian sects in the seventeenth century, the Quakers were the least obsessed with history, the least addicted to the idolatry of things in time. They believed that the inner light was in all human beings and that salvation came to those who lived in conformity with that light and was not dependent on the profession of beliefs in historical or pseudo-historical events, nor on the performance of certain rites, nor on the support of a particular ecclesiastical organization.[2]

Aldous Huxley

GEORGE FOX'S CALL

The first time we know of George Fox coming to the notice of authority was in 1649, when he was imprisoned in Nottingham. This was at a crucial point of the English revolution, the year in which King Charles I was executed and the Puritan attempt to enforce morality by legislation began to gain impetus. We should remember that the idea of political revolution did not then have the familiarity which it has since acquired; although in England there were radical movements among ordinary people, such as the Levellers. (One of their leaders, John Lilburne, joined the Quakers, the Society Fox was to found.) The scientific revolution of ideas had not yet spread; Galileo's *Dialogue on the Great World Systems,* published in 1632, had instantly been suppressed, and Newton was only seven years old. But the revolution in religious thought which had challenged the monolithic mediaeval church and produced the Reformation was over a hundred years old. The years of the Commonwealth in England were a time of extreme and independent views, bitter controversy, and uncertainty about the nature of religious authority. Many groups of people had been abandoned by the established churches or withdrawn from them; generally known as 'Seekers', they waited for a new revelation of God's truth. The religious persecutions of the previous century were still a strong memory (Fox says his mother was 'of the stock of the martyrs'), and the country was emerging from seven years of civil war.

Even in this upheaval, George Fox stood out as a striking and unexpected figure. He was then twenty-five, burly, strong, long-haired (in contrast to the Puritan fashion), peasant-featured, astute. He came from the back of the beyond, the village of Fenny Drayton in Leicestershire, where he had been working for a man who kept sheep and dealt in wool and hides; his teaching sometimes draws on his experience as a shepherd. His handwriting was laboured, his spelling eccentric even for those days, and most of his later writing was dictated to others.

He had left home and job when he was nineteen, and began to travel from place to place, seeking a religious teacher who could give him some assurance of truth. But he found none till, in 1647, at the deepest point of his disillusionment with all human instructors, he records that he heard a voice say to him: 'There is One, even Christ Jesus, that can speak to thy condition'.[3] This crowned his religious sensitivity with a certainty that seldom left him.

For over a year he seems to have worked on the implications of this message or insight. If Jesus could speak to him, directly, when all those who were experienced in the Bible and theology had failed to communicate, this cast serious doubts on the claims which the churches made for their organization and ministry—doubts which others were feeling at the same time. But how else was divine guidance to be sought? Re-reading his Bible, he found line after line coming alive with new meaning and relevance. He expresses this by saying he was 'in the same Spirit' as its authors when they wrote it. This was not a claim that every word was inspired; Fox came to see clearly that there is a progressing teaching in the Bible which culminated in the message of Jesus.

He writes: 'And the scriptures—some of them are history done in their times when they were written, and some of them are shadows and figurative and typical of things in their times—of which Christ is the substance and end. So the scriptures of truth is the best book upon earth to be read, believed, fulfilled and practised . . .'[4]

We can compare his experience with the flash of intuition with which we recognise the truth in a piece of writing which we previously found obscure, the sudden sense of being in deep communication with another mind. But I think we must concede that Fox's experience went still deeper, in that these were not scattered insights, but each new 'opening' (as he calls them) was found to relate to one single Truth for which he found, like Dante, that the most suitable metaphor was 'the Light'. 'Within the depths of the eternal light,' writes Dante, 'I saw gathered into one book by love the pages which are scattered through the universe; substance and qualities and their relationships fused together in such a way that what I speak of is one single flame.'[5] And Fox: 'I saw also that there was an ocean of darkness and death, but an infinite ocean of light and love, which flowed over the ocean of darkness.'[6]

He had to search out how he came by this understanding. There was no doubt in his mind that it came of the Grace of God (though at one time he toyed with the speculation that all things came by nature, till he was quite 'overclouded' by it). He began to feel that many of the practices of religion, as he had known them, had been obstacles in his search; it was only as he stopped clinging to them that real experience and understanding came. He would have agreed with Paul Tillich: 'I think of the theologian who does not wait for God, because he possesses Him, enclosed within a doctrine. I think of the biblical student who does not wait for God because he possesses Him, enclosed in a book. I think of the churchman who does not wait for God because he possesses Him, enclosed in an institution.'[7]

So it was that in 1649, already the centre of a like-minded group, he felt God wanted him to go into the church at Nottingham. The priest was no doubt trying to urge his flock to stand firm despite the bewildering religious controversies of the times, and he told them to use the scriptures as the test of all religious opinions. George Fox cried out against this, pointing out that the Jews had tested Christ's teachings against the scriptures, and yet they crucified him. While he was developing his account of the Holy Spirit he was arrested in the church, and endured the first of his eight imprisonments. In prison he converted the sheriff who had charge of him to his way of thinking; this man and his family took Fox out of prison to live with them, till the authorities objected and sent him back.

On this occasion, he was released without examination or trial. But the following year he was brought before the magistrates at Derby for blasphemy, and spent over a year in prison there. There were a fair number of religious 'enthusiasts' in England in those days. They were often tolerated or even respected, and this kind of persecution was unsystematic, depending on local prejudice. Indeed the Quaker movement was fortunate in having these years of the Commonwealth in which to develop its teaching and increase in numbers before meeting a storm of organized persecution in the 1660s. Much of this early harassment was due to superficial irritation or unfounded rumour; for instance George Fox was said to be a witch. But there was a core of profound revolution in his spiritual teaching, which must have alarmed any of his hearers who carried religious authority. It is to this we must now turn.

In a passage from his Journal relating to 1648, he sets out his message:

> I was glad that I was commanded to turn people to that Inward Light, Spirit and Grace, by which all might know their salvation and their way to God; even that divine Spirit which would lead them into all Truth and which I infallibly knew would never deceive any. But with and by this divine Power and Spirit of God, and the Light of Jesus, I was to bring people off from all their own ways to Christ, the new and living Way; and from their churches, which men had made and gathered, to the Church in God, the general assembly written in Heaven, which Christ is the Head of; and off from the world's teachers made by men, to learn of Christ, who is the Way, the Truth and the Life, of whom the Father said: 'This is my beloved Son, hear ye him'; and off from all the world's worships, to know the Spirit of Truth in the inward parts, and to be led thereby, that in it they might worship the Father of spirits, who seeks such to worship

> him—in which Spirit they that worshipped not knew not what they worshipped.
>
> And I was to bring people off from all the world's religions, which are vain, that they might know the pure religion, and might visit the fatherless, the widows and the strangers, and keep themselves from the spots of the world. And then there would not be so many beggars, the sight of whom often grieved my heart, to see so much hard-heartedness amongst them that professed the name of Christ. And I was to bring them off from all the world's fellowships and prayings and singings, which stood in forms without power, that their fellowships should be in the Holy Ghost and in the eternal Spirit of God, that they might pray in the Holy Ghost and sing in the Spirit and with the Grace that comes by Jesus, making melody in their hearts to the Lord who hath sent his beloved Son to be their Saviour, and caused his heavenly Sun to shine upon all the world and his heavenly Rain to fall upon the just and unjust (as his outward rain doth fall and his outward sun doth shine on all) which is God's unspeakable love to the world.[8]

Almost every leader of a 'religious revival' is critical of established religious practice, and claims he is replacing empty shams with true worship and membership of 'the Church of God'. Those who are familiar with such movements may feel that Fox's manifesto reads like all the others, and recall how often and how quickly these burnt themselves out in fanaticism or relapsed into a new and still more rigid orthodoxy. It cannot be claimed that Quakers have always avoided these fates; but none the less it is at this point that we can see that Fox was indeed different. Tempted to each extreme in turn, he found his way between them without losing his belief in 'that of God' in each person, without setting himself up as sole arbiter of truth. He is sometimes pictured, even by Quakers today, as an authoritarian church leader, sometimes as a fanatical revivalist. Both images are unjust, and distort our view of an extraordinary and complex man: mystic, revolutionary, prophet and preacher of compelling power, adventurer, self-taught writer, healer (who like Jesus sometimes did not wait to see the result), advocate of new ideas (including equal treatment for men and women, abolition of the death penalty, conservative use of natural resources, workschemes for the unemployed, and the necessity for doctors to understand the mind and spirit as well as the body), organiser and democrat (the last word being quite inadequate to encompass the decision-making process developed by Friends, which will be described later).

Religious visionaries are sometimes thought to be impractical; but George Fox—like many of them—had a robust common sense. He was also somewhat authoritarian by temperament, which is something quite apart from the authority which his spiritual stature gave him. We shall be able to see him struggling with this temperament and the temptations it brought him, and conquering them, so that William Penn who knew him well towards the end of his life could write of him: 'He exercised no authority but over evil, and that everywhere and in all, but with love, compassion and long-suffering . . .'*—Fox was in no doubt where the source of authority lay, and that everyone could know it without intermediary.

Although he protested against the formal and dogmatic elements in the religious teaching and practice of his day, he used the traditional language of theology, which may now seem outdated or unfamiliar to some readers. The religious debates of his time had the advantage of this agreed vocabulary, the language of the Bible. Its translation and mass-printing were much nearer them than us, its words still fresh, strong and expressive. For many of us this language has now been so debased that it no longer gives us the words in which to talk about experiences which are intensely meaningful to us, and much more widespread than is sometimes supposed. Fortunately there is also a grandeur in much of his writing which

* See pages 104–6.

can speak to us directly, so that in my comments I need not feel that I keep coming between the reader and this extraordinary man.

Here are some extracts from his accounts of his first spiritual experiences, and his rejection of what he found to be artificial and empty.

* * *

'Put not your trust in any child of man, for there is no help in them'

Now after I had received that opening from the Lord that to be bred at Oxford or Cambridge was not sufficient to fit a man to be a minister of Christ, I regarded the priests less, and looked more after the dissenting people. And among them I saw there was some tenderness, and many of them came afterwards to be convinced, for they had some openings. But as I had forsaken all the priests, so I left the separate preachers also, and those called the most experienced people; for I saw there was none among them all that could speak to my condition. And when all my hopes in them and in all men were gone, so that I had nothing outwardly to help me, nor could tell me what to do, then, O then, I heard a voice which said 'There is one, even Christ Jesus, that can speak to thy condition'. And when I heard it my heart did leap for joy. Then the Lord did let me see why there was none upon the earth that could speak to my condition, namely that I might give him all the glory; for all are concluded under sin, and shut up in unbelief as I had been, that Jesus Christ might have the pre-eminence, who enlightens, and gives grace, and faith, and power. Thus, when God doth work, who shall let it?* And this I knew experimentally.

Journal (1647) p. 11†

* i.e. who shall hinder it?
† See Note on Sources, p. 117.

Spiritual experiences as a young man

I was often under great temptations; and I fasted much and walked abroad in solitary places many days, and often took my Bible and went and sat in hollow trees and lonesome places till night came on; and frequently in the night walked mournfully about by myself, for I was a man of sorrows in the times of the first workings of the Lord in me . . .

And when I myself was in the deep, under all shut up, I could not believe that I should ever overcome; my troubles, my sorrows and my temptations, were so great, that I thought many times I should have despaired, I was so tempted.

Journal (1647) pp. 9 and 12

Now was I come up in spirit through the flaming sword into the paradise of God. All things were new, and all the creation gave another smell unto me than before, beyond what words can utter. I knew nothing but pureness, and innocency, and righteousness, being renewed up into the image of God by Christ Jesus, so that I say I was come up to the state of Adam which he was in before he fell. The creation was opened to me, and it was showed me how all things had their names given them according to their nature and virtue. And I was at a stand in my mind whether I should practice physic for the good of mankind, seeing the nature and virtues of the creatures were opened to me by the Lord. But I was immediately taken up in spirit, to see into another or more steadfast state than Adam's in innocency, even into a state in Christ Jesus, that should never fall.

Journal (1648) p. 27

The scriptures and the Light of Truth

I saw that Christ had died for all men, and was a propitiation for all, and had enlightened all men and women with his divine and saving Light, and that none could be a true believer but who believed in it. I saw that the Grace of God, which brings salvation, had appeared to all men, and that the manifestation of the Spirit of God was given to every man to profit withal. These things I did not see by the help of man, nor by the letter, though they are written in the letter, but I saw them in the Light of the Lord Jesus Christ, and by his Spirit and Power, as did the holy men of God by whom the Holy Scriptures were written. Yet I had no slight esteem of the Holy Scriptures, but they were very precious to me, for I was in that spirit by which they were given forth, and what the Lord opened in me I afterwards found was agreeable to them.

Journal (1648) p. 34

Now as I passed to Nottingham on a First-Day in the morning with Friends to a meeting, which I came on top of a hill, as I looked upon the town the great steeplehouse struck at my life when I spied it, a great idol and idolatrous temple. And the Lord said unto me, 'Thou must go cry against yonder great idol and against the worshippers therein.' So I said nothing of this to the Friends that were with me, but went on with them to the meeting, where the mighty power of the Lord God was amongst us, in which I left Friends sitting in the meeting, and I went away to the steeplehouse.

And when I came there, all the people looked like fallow ground, and the priest like a great lump of earth stood in his pulpit above. He took for his text these words of Peter, 'We have also a more sure word of prophecy, whereunto ye do well that ye take heed, as unto a light that shineth in a dark place, until the day dawn and the day-star arise in your hearts'. And he told the people that the scriptures were the touch-stone and judge by which they were to try all doctrines, religions and opinions, and to end controversy.

Now the Lord's power was so mighty upon me, and so strong in me, that I could not hold, but was made to cry out and say, 'Oh, no, it is not the scriptures', and was commanded to tell them God did not dwell in temples made with hands. But I told them what it was, namely the Holy Spirit, by which the holy men of God gave forth the scriptures, whereby opinions, religions, and judgements were to be tried; for it led into all Truth, and so gave knowledge of all Truth. For the Jews had the scriptures, and yet resisted the Holy Ghost, and rejected Christ the bright morning star; and they persecuted Christ and his apostles and took upon them to try their doctrines by the scriptures, but erred in judgement and did not try them aright, because they tried without the Holy Ghost. Now as I spoke thus amongst them, the officers came and took me away and put me into prison, a pitiful stinking place . . .

Journal (1649) p. 39

'All the world could do me no good'

And I found that there were two thirsts in me, the one after the creatures, to have gotten health and strength there, and the other after the Lord the Creator and his son Jesus Christ. And I saw all the world could do me no good. If I had had a king's diet, palace and attendance, all would have been as nothing, for nothing gave me comfort but the Lord by his power. And I saw professors,* priests and people were whole and at ease in that condition which was my misery, and they loved that which I would have been rid of. But the Lord did stay my desires upon himself from whom my help came, and my care was cast upon him alone. Therefore all wait patiently upon the Lord, whatsoever condition you be in; wait in the Grace and Truth that comes by Jesus; for if ye do so, there is a promise to you, and the Lord God will fulfil it in you.

Journal (1647) p. 12

My travails have been great, in hungers and colds, when there were few [of us], for the first six or seven years; that I often lay in woods and on commons in the night; that many times it was as a byword, that I would not come into their houses and lie in their

* i.e. professing Christians.

beds; and the prisons have been made my home a great part of my time, and I have been in danger of my life, and in jeopardy daily. And amongst you [fellow Quakers] I have made myself of no reputation, to keep the Truth up in reputation, as you all very well know that are in the fear of God. With the low I made myself low; and with the weak and feeble I was as one with them and condescended to all conditions; for the Lord fitted me to do so before he sent me forth; and so I passed through great sufferings in my body, as you have been sensible.

Epistle 308 (1674)

Would Christ be received by his Church today?

And now, priests and proud prelates, and bishops and popes, though you have made a trade of the saints' words, and the apostles' and prophets' words, and gotten a great deal of money by them; yet, nevertheless, if a company of shepherds, herdsmen, fishermen, tent-makers, and toll-gatherers should come amongst you to preach, you would say, Away with these mechanic fellows! they have not served seven years' apprenticeship at the colleges which were set up to make ministers . . . Would you own Christ if he had come in your day, who was called a carpenter's son? You popes with your triple crowns, and you lord bishops, with your coaches and pampered horses, and gorgeous apparel, with your black coats and white coats, and silk girdles—are you like to entertain him who was called a carpenter's son; or to cast him and his mother into the manger in your stables?

Epistle 249 (1667)

Evil is reproved by the life of the good man

Live in the Life, and in the Seed, the Power and Righteousness that is everlasting . . . in which ye come to live the life which is well-pleasing to God; a life which shall stand when the world is ended. And in this Life, Power and Wisdom of God, that is endless, you are a terror to all that be in the wisdom below; you are a terror to all that be in unrighteous actions and words; and you are a terror to all that be in the unjust and unequal doings, and all the defrauders, cozeners, cheaters, over-reachers, liars and wrong-dealers. In the Power of God and his Life in which ye have justice, ye have truth, ye have equity, ye have righteousness; and it cometh to be to you as natural. Your words, your lives, your conversations, your presence, and your practices, both judge and preach.

The Line of Righteousness and Justice (1661) p. 7

THE PERSONAL AND CORPORATE CONSCIENCE

A girl in Dorset, on her way for the first time to hear George Fox preach, found herself thinking, 'What is it that condemns me when I do evil, and justifies me when I do well? What is it?' After a while in the meeting, George Fox stood up and said: 'Who art thou that queriest in thy mind, What is it I feel which condemneth me when I do evil, and justifieth me when I do well? I will tell thee. Lo! He that formed the mountains and created the winds, and declareth unto man what are his thoughts, that maketh the morning darkness and treadeth upon the high places of the earth; the Lord, the Lord of Hosts is his name. It is He, by his Spirit, that condemneth thee for evil, and justifieth thee when thou dost well. Keep under its dictates, and He will be thy preserver to the end.'[9]

This story brings beautifully together a number of the strands which confirmed for the early Friends their experience of God within themselves. Not conscience itself, which is a human faculty, but the Light which illuminates it; the awareness of truth and love and beauty in the deep parts of our minds; the sense of the power of nature, which many of us feel more intensely in 'the high places of the earth'; the impetus ('dictate') to action which sometimes comes most inconveniently, against our obvious interests and conscious wishes, but which we ignore at the cost of our peace of mind; the almost miraculous sympathy with the feelings and thoughts of another, which most of us know rarely, but Fox had to a high degree: all these are familiar to agnostic and 'irreligious' people. But Fox calls us to recognize them as the traces of 'that of God' in us, and to identify them with the God revealed in the Bible, 'the Lord of Hosts', working through his Spirit.

If this is true, we shall want to ask how it is that the record of human history is so poor, and why our own lives are so confused and halting. This is of course the great question for the theologians of every religion, and not just an objection to Quaker beliefs. But Friends appealed to experience rather than theological doctrine. They might answer: 'If I experience my own life (or human history) as confused and unsatisfactory, why is this? Why do the satisfactions which I seek not make me happy? Why does my friend with less money and more troubles have a sense of the meaning of life which I lack? Why do I feel obscurely guilty about things which I have a perfect right to do for myself? Where do the standards derive from by which I measure this guilt and confusion? Why can I not hold on to the meaning of those moments when I feel free and in harmony with everything about me? Doesn't a large part of my dissatisfaction come from an awareness of something beyond the values which I allow to rule my life?'

This kind of dis-ease, so far as one can judge, has always been a common experience. To assuage it men turn to religious practices and doctrines; and when they are 'tender' (in Fox's terminology), they can be led through these to the reality which gives them meaning. But this reality, experienced in the heart, demands changes in our lives. If we are not willing, through fear or selfishness, to make these changes, religious observance becomes more like an attempt to buy off our consciences. Even a code of morality can be a defence against acknowledging the 'holiness of the heart's affections'. For these reasons, Fox fiercely opposed the church of his day, deeply involved in the exploitation of the poor, social control and political bloodshed. His harshest words are for its representatives, and his greatest sense of triumph is when he brings one of them reluctantly to 'confess the Truth'. We may find a parallel with Jesus' attitude to some manifestations of organized religion and its representatives.

What difference would it make to our actions if we really

believed that there was something of God in every person with whom we had dealings? And would this be different in effect from a humanistic belief in the unique value of each person? I would like to deal with these questions obliquely at first by turning back to the practice of George Fox and the early Friends (for whom, of course, the term 'God' was not in question). They felt they must witness to the equality of all humankind, male and female, heathen and Christian, lay and clerical, peasant, bourgeois and aristocrat. This was shown individually and as a group in caring attitudes towards beggars, prisoners, servants and slaves, the sick and insane (areas in which Friends later contributed notably towards human progress). They also refused to use the customary signs of respect towards the powerful—such as the deferential 'you' for 'thou', and taking off their hats. Later historians, notably Macaulay, had their fun at this; but Friends experienced angry reactions which showed that their intentions were well understood. George Fox reveals his dry sense of humour when he writes:

> Oh, the blows, punchings, beatings and imprisonments that we underwent for not putting our hats off to men! For that soon tried all men's patience and sobriety what it was. Some had their hats violently plucked off and thrown away so that they quite lost them. The bad language and evil usage we received on this account are hard to be expressed, besides the danger we were sometimes in of losing our lives for this matter, and that by the great professors of Christianity [that is, professing Christians] who thereby discovered that they were not true believers.[10]

The Quaker belief in the equality and brotherhood of all men caused difficulties for the many soldiers who adopted it. George Fox refused the offer of a captaincy in Cromwell's army as early as 1651, saying that he 'lived in the virtue of that life and power that took away the occasion of all wars'. But for many of the others, it was the issue of army authority and discipline which first caused difficulties and got them discharged. Gradually the insight grew that the carrying and use of weapons, warfare, and even the death penalty, were contrary to the witness of God in their hearts and the recorded teaching of Jesus. In the troubled year between Cromwell's death and the restoration of Charles II, Quakers refused the positions they were offered by the Committee of Safety to help in ensuring public order, partly for political reasons, but also because violence might be involved.

Friends' attitude to the secular authority was that they should respect the law in so far as it did not conflict with their direct apprehension of the law of Christ; and if they had to break it, they willingly accepted the consequences, refusing to pay a fine or accept a pardon, in witness to the fact that they were doing what they knew to be right. They fearlessly sought out those in authority and spoke to them frankly, as equals. Fox met Cromwell several times and harangued him about the responsibilities of government as well as the sufferings of persecuted Friends. It is a tribute to Fox's personality that both Cromwell and Charles II showed respect for him as well as curiosity. And when the opportunity arose in New Jersey and Pennsylvania to set up governments based on Quaker principles, the challenge was taken up and boldly carried through.

None the less Friends often suffered at the hands of these same authorities, and a number died in prison. These experiences brought them close to prisoners and outcasts, and also tested their Christian love and forbearance towards their judges, guards and gaolers. On many occasions these people were won over from enmity and ridicule to respect and trust. For a belief in 'that of God in every man' asserts that if we act towards another person, even an oppressor, in the Spirit of Christ, we may reach and awaken the same Spirit in him. Thus Quakers anticipated some of the beliefs and techniques of

Gandhi, using 'soul-force' to create peace in violent situations.

> And so we went to our inn again, and there were two desperate fellows fighting so that none durst come nigh to part them; but I was moved in the Lord's power to go to them, and when I had loosed their hands I held one by one hand and one by the other hand; and I showed them the evil of their doings and convinced them and reconciled them to each other that they were loving and very thankful . . .[11]

But Gandhi used 'non-violence' to political ends, and was troubled by the element of coercion it involved. Fox's acts of reconciliation, and his response to oppression, were disinterested.

At all times the Quaker had to witness to the Spirit of God within him, knowing that his words or actions might be God's means of awakening this Spirit in a fellow man or woman. If he kept a shop, he must show an equal honesty to all; and his customers discovered that they could even send a child to buy from him without his cheating or adjusting his prices and weights. (This fair dealing often drew trade away from competitors—another reason for denigrating the Quakers!) If he was a craftsman, his work must be sound but simple, not encouraging worldly vanity. If he was a labourer he must give his employer full and honest service, yet show him the respect due to an equal, not a superior.

But also, like the Old Testament prophet, the Quaker might be called to apparently irrational actions. He lived in an age when the traditional structures and beliefs in religion and politics (seen as fundamentally one) were challenged by groups such as the Diggers, Levellers, Familists and Ranters. Some of these groups developed an extreme emotional fervour and a moral individualism which acknowledged no commandments. Many looked for the ending of the world. Friends had to discover where they stood in relation to this, all the more because they attracted adherents from these groups. In the early years some Quakers 'went naked in the streets for a sign', wrought miracles or prophesied coming disasters. The records abound in actions taken in obedience to interior promptings. Some of these turned out to be crucial, either for the Quaker movement, or to the fate of an individual. At times there was no visible outcome, as when George Fox walked barefoot through Lichfield crying, 'Woe to the bloody city!' But though this action was uncharacteristic, and contrary to his down-to-earth common sense, he had no embarrassment at recording it in his Journal. But when he was 'moved' to climb Pendle Hill and 'sound the day of the Lord' on the top of it to the empty air, he was rewarded with a vision of a people in white raiment waiting to be gathered in the North West. His action in response to this vision led to a great and fruitful expansion of the Quaker movement.

The same sense of God was shown in more considered actions: those for example of Mary Fisher, a servant girl from Yorkshire who sailed to Turkey and, incredibly, secured an interview with the Sultan of the Ottoman Empire to speak to him as an ambassador from God; or William Penn, who founded the State of Pennsylvania and set up its constitution on principles which included no army or militia, no death penalty, and respect for the rights of American Indians as equals.

Speech as well as action had to be open to the Spirit's inspiration. It was of paramount importance to say what one knew to be true. Friends refused to speak on oath, because this would have implied that their everyday utterances were untrustworthy. Incidentally, this gave magistrates an almost certain way of committing them to prison, because if a Friend was asked to take the Oath of Allegiance, which could be administered to anyone to prove he was a true subject of the realm, the answer would be No. As with so many of their insights, there were two paths to this conclusion: by following in action the logic of their principles; and by taking seriously the

New Testament ('Swear not at all', and 'Let your Yea be Yea and your Nay, Nay'). As we have seen, Fox did not regard the Bible as the fountain of Truth; but its writings flowed from this fountain, as did the inspired actions and words of Friends, so it was natural that they should generally be in accord.

When Charles II asked one of the first Quakers, 'How did you come to believe the Scriptures were true?' the answer was, 'I have believed the Scriptures from a child to be a declaration of truth, when I had but a literal knowledge, education and tradition; but now I know the Scriptures to be true by the manifestations and operation of God fulfilling them in me.'[12]

This is a very large claim, but it is supported time and again by the quality of the teaching and writing of Fox and his immediate friends and fellow workers. (In view of the independence with which they acted, it is inappropriate to call them 'followers'.) Most of them at the beginnings were humble men and women, and few of them had much education. I wonder whether there has been a group since the days of Jesus' apostles so unlikely, from a worldly point of view, to have provided a great enrichment and re-interpretation of Christianity. And yet, when one re-reads the Sermon on the Mount in the light of their teaching and experiences, it seems appropriate, perhaps even inevitable, that new light should have come from such men. Their writings are uneven in quality (as are Fox's); but they contain many passages of great beauty and inspiration, out of experience unmistakably personal. (To show something of what Fox could awake in men, I have included some of these passages in this book.)

The Quaker claim was not limited to a small number of enthusiasts. By the time of George Fox's death in 1691, one Englishman in every hundred was a Quaker, worshipping in a way which had almost no point of contact with the other churches' traditions. They were the largest of the dissenting sects. Their movement was equally remarkable for its courage, its toleration, its discipline and its democracy. In 'steeple-houses', lawcourts, shops and streets, in and out of prison, in prosperity and under threat of death, among the humble and before the powerful, they witnessed to a direct experience of God which changed the way they lived their lives. We find this not only in the heroic lives of the founders and missionaries, whose deeds are recorded at length, but in many anecdotes which throw a brief light on obscurer Friends in their homes and local communities.

A sceptic might say that there is no way to distinguish this alleged divine guidance from self-willed individualism. We shall have to look at this objection both psychologically and historically later in this book. But one might start to answer it by saying that early Friends found that their experience bore out the scripture: 'He will guide you into all Truth'.[13] That is, they expected to find that the insight given by the Spirit to one man could not contradict that given to another; nor could it disagree with the teaching of Jesus. Fox wrote, 'All they that are in the Light are in unity; for the Light is but one'.[14] And he quotes from *Jeremiah*:

> But this shall be the covenant that I will make with the house of Israel: After those days, saith the Lord, I will put my law in their inward parts and write it in their hearts; and will be their God, and they shall be my people. And they shall teach no more every man his neighbour, and every man his brother, saying, Know the Lord: for they shall all know me, from the least of them unto the greatest of them, saith the Lord; for I will forgive their iniquity, and I will remember their sin no more.[15]

Any disagreement, whether over a course of action or a matter of belief, could only indicate that one or more parties to the discussion had not yet clearly perceived the truth. In practice a tension, which can be very fruitful, has always existed in Quaker experience between the conviction of the individual and the consensus of the group of Friends gathered together. All men have personal interests, desires, fears and prejudices which can drown the interior voice of Truth. Friends evolved very quickly a unique method of worship and discussion; it begins, ends and is interspersed with silence; its participants searching for the will of God to be done, not their own will. They try to put personal considerations aside, listen to one another with the respect due to God himself, and let anger and misunderstanding ebb away in the silence. If any member cannot agree to a certain decision, the group will not proceed with it; but equally the individual whenever possible is required to test his 'leadings of the Spirit' by bringing them to the group.

This desire to harmonize the individual vision with the corporate wisdom of the meeting was not easy. Painful experience (of which I shall relate a little) played a part in drawing the line. But it is still characteristic of Friends today. It is now relevant to the seeking of many others who want to give expression to their personal intuitions and at the same time find a group to which to relate. But the Quaker insight goes beyond the need for an authority either to follow or reject. Nor does it offer scope for self-willed individuality, like the permissive strands in today's culture which lay moral responsibility on the individual but offer few guidelines beyond honesty in relationships and the right to gratification. Quaker self-fulfilment is a discipline, founded on a conviction that God's will can be found when we lay aside our own; that if it becomes clear to only one man in a gathering, the others will recognize it when they listen to him in this spirit; and this will is single in a given situation, not diverse or self-contradictory.

One early Quaker writer described such meetings in these words:

> When I came into the silent assemblies of God's people, I felt a secret power among them, which touched my heart; and as I gave way unto it I found the evil weakening in me and the good raised up; and so I became thus knit and united

> to them, hungering more and more after the increase of this power and life whereby I might feel myself perfectly redeemed; and indeed this is the surest way to become a Christian . . .[16]

Others, more simply, have felt in their meetings the confirmation of the promise of Jesus, 'Where two or three are gathered together in my name, there am I also in the midst of them'.

* * *

Christ the Teacher

We had a general meeting of many thousands of people a-top of a hill. Heavenly and glorious it was and the glory of the Lord did shine over all . . . Their eyes were kept to Christ their Teacher and they came to sit under their Vine, that afterwards a Friend in the ministry, Francis Howgill, went amongst them, and when he was moved to stand up amongst them he saw they had no need of words for they was all sitting down under their Teacher Christ Jesus; so he was moved to sit down again amongst them without speaking anything.

Journal (1653) p. 168

Is not Christ said to be a shepherd? Is not that an office, to look to his sheep? It is the office and work of an outward shepherd to look to the outward sheep and help them out of the briars and brambles, to help them out of the pits and ponds, and to feed them in pastures and drive them to the springs and brooks to drink. So Christ is the heavenly shepherd and pulls his sheep out of the pit of old Adam and his brambles, briars and thorns, and brings them to the pastures of life. They, his sheep, know his voice and he goes before them and gives them life eternal, life abundantly and brings them to the river of life and springs of life, where he waters his flock which lie down at noonday. They follow the footsteps of the flock, their path is a shining light. So Christ is a shepherd in the midst of his people which he gathers in his name. He exercises the office of a shepherd in the midst of them in their hearts. And when their minds go astray, he plucks them back again with his heavenly crook and so keeps the soul and mind from the dogs, wolves, ravening beasts and devouring fowls, and keeps the soul and spirit upon the pastures of life and springs of life. O Blessed Shepherd for ever!

A collected set of passages from George Fox's writings, edited to be read aloud by Hugh McGregor Ross (Unpublished, available Friends House Library, London)

I let them see their true teacher . . . and how the Lord was come to teach his people himself; and the Light which Christ did enlighten withal, they might come to in themselves, and so by it come to Christ.

Journal (1651) p. 80

All men have access to God's truth

And now, Friends, we understand that some that have come lately among you have been under great sufferings and abuses by their Patrons, because they cannot honour them with that honour as other slaves do, or as they have done before. Now, if you wait in patience upon the Lord in his Truth (for you are to buy the Truth, and not to sell it; and Truth is that that's stronger than all), the Lord in his time (though he may try you) can mollify that nature in them there, as he hath done in other places where he hath tried his people with such things. And when your [Turkish] captors hath seen 'tis for conscience sake towards God, and it is from the principle of Truth and the Spirit—in which Spirit and Truth they worship the Most High God, who is an eternal incomprehensible Spirit, who is God in Heaven and God in the Earth, and dwells by his Spirit in his humble people—they have been overcome.

'To the Meeting of Friends in Truth, that are captives in Algiers'.

Epistle 391 (1684)

Concerning religion, we believe that it is only this Spirit of the Lord that makes men truly religious; and that no man ought to be compelled to or from any exercise in religion, by any outward law or power; but every man ought to be left free, as the Lord shall persuade his own mind, in doing or leaving undone this or the other practice in religion; and every man, of what profession in religion soever, ought to be protected in peace, provided himself be a man of peace, not seeking the wrong of any man's person or estate . . . And we believe that Christ is and ought only to be Lord and exerciser of men's consciences; and his Spirit only must lead into all Truth.

Edward Burrough, *A Declaration to all the World of our Faith* (1657)

I had a meeting at Shelter Island among the Red Indians on the 1st day of the 6th month. Their king and council with about 100 more Indians with him sat about two hours, and I spoke to them by an interpreter that was an Indian that could speak any English very well. They sat down like Friends and appeared very loving; they said all was Truth and did make a confession of it after the meeting. So I have set up a meeting among them once a fortnight, and a Friend, Joseph Sylvester, is to read the Scriptures to them, Negroes and Indians.

Journal (1672) p. 625

Attacked by the people of Ulverston

Then the rude people said to the Justice, 'Give him us!' and he did. So of a sudden all the people in the steeplehouse were in an outrage and an uproar, that they fell upon me in the steeplehouse before his face, with staves and fists and books, and knocked me down and kicked me and trampled upon me. And many people tumbled over their seats for fear and were knocked down, and the Justice and the priests among them. And at last the Justice said among the rude people, 'Give him me!' and he came and took me from amongst the people again and led me out of the steeple-house and put me into the hands of four officers and constables, and bid them whip me and put me out of the town. And they led me about a quarter of a mile, some taking hold by my collar and some by the arms and shoulders and shook me by the head, and some by the hands, and dragged me through mire and dirt and water. And many friendly people that were come to the market, and some into the steeplehouse to hear me, many of them they knocked down, and broke their heads also. And the blood ran down several people so as I never saw the like in my life as I looked at them, when they were dragging me along. And Judge Fell's son running after to see what they would do with me, they threw him into a ditch of water and cried, 'Knock the teeth out of his head!' And some got staves and some got hedge stakes and some got holme bushes and some got willows.

And when they had led me to the common moss, and a multitude of people following, the constables took me and gave me a wisk over the shoulders with their willow rods, and so thrust me amongst the rude multitude which then fell upon me with their hedge stakes and clubs and staves, and beat me as hard as ever they could strike on my head and arms and shoulders and it was a great while before they beat me down and mazed me, and at last I fell down upon the wet common. There I lay a pretty space, and when I recovered myself again, and saw myself lying on a watery common and all the people standing about me, I lay a little still, and the power of the Lord sprang through me, and the eternal refreshings refreshed me, that I stood up again in the eternal power of God and stretched out my arms amongst them all, and said again with a loud voice, 'Strike again, here is my arms and my head and my cheeks.' And there was a mason, a rude fellow, a professor called, he gave me a blow with all his might just a-top of my hand, as it was stretched out, with his walking rule-staff. And my hand and arm was so numbed and bruised that I could not draw it in unto me again but it stood out as it was. Then the people cried out, 'He hath spoiled his hand, for ever having any use of it more.' The skin was struck off my hand and a little blood came, and I looked at it in the love of God, and I was in the love of God to them all that had persecuted me.

And after a while the Lord's power sprang through me again, and through my hand and arm, that in a minute I recovered my hand and arm and strength, in the face and sight of them all, and it was as well as it was before, and I never had another blow afterward.

And then they began to fall out among themselves, and some of them came to me and said if I would give them money they would secure me from the rest; but I denied it, and was moved of the Lord to declare unto them the word of life, and showed them their false Christianity, and the fruits of their priests, and how they were more like heathens and Jews and not like Christians. And they said if I came into the town again they would kill me.

And so I was moved of the Lord to come up again through them, and up into Ulverston market and there meets me a man with a sword, a soldier. 'Sir,' said he, 'I am your servant, I am ashamed that you should be thus abused, for you are a man,' said he. He was grieved and said he would assist me in what he could, and I told him it was no matter, the Lord's power was over all.

And so as I walked through the people in the market there was none of them had power to touch me. And this man with his sword was walking after me and some of the market people were striking up of Friends' heels in the market and I turned me about and I saw the soldier amongst them with his naked rapier; and I run amongst them and catched hold of his hand that the rapier was in and bid him put up his sword again if he would come along with me, for I was willing to draw him out from the company, lest some mischief should be done.

And so he came to the town's end with me.

Journal (1652) p. 127

To live in peace is to live in Christ

All that pretend to fight for Christ, they are deceived, for his kingdom is not of this world, therefore his servants do not fight. Therefore fighters are not of Christ's Kingdom, but are without Christ's Kingdom; for his Kingdom stands in peace and righteousness, but fighters are in the lust, and all that would destroy men's lives are not of Christ's mind, who came to save men's lives . . . All such as pretend Christ Jesus and confess him, and yet run into the use of carnal weapons, wrestling with flesh and blood, throw away the spiritual weapons . . .

All Friends everywhere, this I charge you, which is the word of the Lord God unto you all, live in peace, in Christ, the way of peace, and therein seek the peace of all men, and no man's hurt. As I said before, in Adam in the Fall is no peace, but in Adam out of the Fall, in him is peace; so, ye being in Adam which never fell, it is love that overcomes, and not hatred with hatred, nor strife with strife. Therefore live all in the peaceable life, doing good to all men and seeking the good and welfare of all men.

Letter to Friends in *Journal* (1659) p. 357

Challenges and answers in prison

And there were two bad prisoners that often would drink with the officers and soldiers, and because I would not sit and drink with them they made them worse against me. One time when they were almost drunk, one of them, Will Wilkinson, a Presbyterian who had been a captain, came and challenged me to fight with him. And they were both full of beer, and when one would be at me the other withheld him, and when the other would be at me then the other would withhold him. And the next morning when they were more sober I told him that challenged me I was come to answer him, with my hands in my pockets, and reaching back my head towards him, said there was my hair and my back, and what a shame it was for him to challenge a man whose principle he knew was not to strike; he should have challenged some of the soldiers that might have answered him again. But he skipped away and went into another room, at which the soldiers fell a-laughing, and one of the officers said, 'You are a happy man that can bear such things.'

Journal (1665) p. 493

After this, my wife went to London and spoke to the King, laying before him my long and unjust imprisonment . . . that I being now his prisoner, it was in his power and at his pleasure to release, which she desired. The King spoke kindly to her, and referred her to the lord-keeper, to whom she went, but could not obtain what she desired; for he said the King could not release me otherwise than by a pardon; and I was not free to receive a pardon, knowing I had not done evil. If I would have been freed by a pardon, I need not have laid so long, for the King was willing to give me pardon long before, and told Thomas Moore that I need not scruple being released by a pardon, for many a man that was as innocent as a child had had a pardon granted him. Yet I could not consent to have one. For I had rather have lain in prison all my days than have come out in any way dishonourable to truth.

Journal (1675) p. 701

Quaker dealings with the 'world'

At first ye know that many [of you] could not take so much money in your trade as to buy bread with; all people stood aloof of you when you stood upright . . . But now you, through the Light, come to answer that of God in all, they say they will trust you before their own people, knowing you will not cheat nor wrong nor cozen nor oppress them. For the cry is now amongst them that are without, 'Where is there a Quaker of such and such a trade?' So they will deal with Friends before they will deal with their own.

Oh! therefore, Friends, who have purchased this through great sufferings, lose not this great favour which God hath given unto you; but that you may answer the Witness of God in every man, which witnesseth to your faithfulness, that they may glorify your Father on your behalf.

Epistle 251 (1667)

Wrong no man, over-reach no man (if it may be never so much to your advantage) but be plain, righteous and holy; in this are ye serviceable to your own nation and others by your change and exchanging of things and merchandize; and to the Lord God ye come to be a blessing in the creation and generation.

And all of what trade and calling soever, keep out of debts, owe no man anything but love . . .

Owe to none anything but love, and in that ye will feel the blessing and come to be serviceable in the creation.

Epistle 200 (1661)

And justices and captains had come to break up this meeting, but when they saw Friends' books and accounts of collections concerning the poor . . . they were made to confess that we did their work, and Friends desired them to come and sit with them then . . .

And many times there would be two hundred beggars of the world there, for all the country knew we met about the poor; wherefore after the meeting was done Friends would send to the bakers and give them each a penny loaf apiece, be they as many as they would; for we were taught to do good to all but especially to the household of faith.

Journal (1660) p. 373

'Take no thought for the morrow'

Oh! be faithful! Look not back, nor be too forward, further than ye have attained; for ye have no time but this present time; therefore prize your time for your soul's sake.

Epistle 5 (1652), to his parents.

King Charles, thou came not into this nation by sword, and not by victory of war, but by the power of the Lord. Now if thou do not live in it, thou wilt not prosper . . .

So hear and consider, and do good in the time whilst thou hast power, and be merciful and forgive; and that is the way to overcome, and obtain the Kingdom of Christ.

G.F.

Letter to Charles II on his accession in *Journal* (1660) p. 368

George Fox in Court

Judge: Sirrah, will you take the oath?

G.F.: I am none of thy sirrahs, I am no sirrah, I am a Christian. Art thou a judge, and sits there and gives ill names to prisoners? It does not become either thy grey hairs or thy office. Thou ought not to give names to prisoners.

Judge: I am a Christian too.

G.F.: Then do Christian works.

Judge: Sirrah, thou thinkest to frighten me with thy words (and looked aside and said, 'I am saying so again.')

G.F.: I speak in love to thee. That doth not become a judge, thou oughtest to instruct a prisoner of the law, and the scripture, if he were ignorant and out of the way.

Judge: George Fox, I speak in love to thee too.

G.F.: Love gives no names.

Judge: Wilt thou swear? Wilt thou take the oath. Yea or nay?

G.F.: As I said before, whether must I obey God or man, judge thee. Christ commands not to swear; and if thee, or you, or any minister or priest here will prove that ever Christ or the apostles, after they had forbidden swearing, commanded that [men] should swear, then I will swear. (And several priests being there, never one appeared or offered to speak.)

Judge: George Fox, will you swear or not?

G.F.: It's in obedience to Christ's command I do not swear;

and for his sake we suffer. And you are sensible enough of swearers how they first swear one way and then another. And if I could take any oath at all upon any occasion, I should take that; but it is not denying oaths upon occasions, but all oaths according to Christ's doctrine . . .

Judge: Then you will not swear. Take him away, gaoler.

G.F.: It is for Christ's sake I cannot swear, and in obedience to his commands I suffer, and so the Lord forgive you all.

Journal (1664) p. 468

The peaceful victory of the Lord

The Peace-Maker hath the Kingdom and is in it; and hath dominion over the peace-breaker, to calm him in the power of God.

Epistle 9 (1652)

Friends never feared their Acts, nor prisons, nor gaols, nor houses of correction, nor banishments, nor spoilings of goods; nay, nor life itself. And there was never any persecution that came, but we saw it was for good; and we looked upon it to be good, as from God; and there never were any prisons that I was in, or sufferings, but still it was for the bringing multitudes more out of prison. For they that imprisoned the Truth and quenched the Spirit in themselves, would prison it and quench it without them. So that there was a time when there were so many in prison that it became a by-word, *Truth was scarcely to be found but in gaols.*

Epistle 2 (1672)

'A Warning to all the Merchants in London'

Your poor and blind and lame cripples and women and children are crying up and down your streets and steeplehouse doors, and alleys and corners, after you that call yourselves Christians, and yet they are Christians as well as you and so members of the same body . . . Yet to let them be crying up and down the streets not provided for, this is to hang gold on one arm and let the other go bare; or to hang gold on the back and let the leg go bare; for all are members of one body, the poor as well as the rich . . .

These things are a grief to many sober people in the city, to see that magistrates have no more feeling of these things, and yet so much profession of religion and preaching among them . . . One might think, if it were but to keep the honour of their city, they would . . . out of their abundance lay a little aside, and have a place provided that all the poor, blind, lame cripples should be put into, and nurses set over them, and looked to, cherished and seen unto that they do not want; and thus they that could work to work . . . that there should not be seen a beggar walk up and down the streets.

You have your many dishes, changes of dishes and that you call novelties—and the poor cannot get bread; spare one of your dishes and let it be carried to the place for the poor, and do not let them come begging for it neither.

Gospel Truth Demonstrated (1706) p. 127

Fishers of Men

Come, fishermen, what have you catched with your nets? What can you say for God? Your brethren Peter and John, fishermen, could say much for God. Read in the Acts and you may see it. I would not have you degenerate from their spirit.

Epistle 275 (1669)

The next day, after the judges were gone out of the town, an order was sent to the gaoler that I should be put in the dungeon amongst the moss-troupers,* and so they did; where men and women were put together and never a house of office,† in a nasty and very uncivil manner which was a shame to

* Moss-troupers: raiders over the Scottish border.
† A house of office: a latrine.

Christianity. And the prisoners were exceeding lousy; and there was one woman eaten almost to death with lice. But the prisoners were made all of them very loving to me, and some of them were convinced, as the publicans and harlots of old were, so that they were able to confound a priest that came to the gates to dispute.

Journal (1653) p. 162

We love all men and women, simply as they are men and women, and as they are God's workmanship, and so as brethren.

Gospel Truth Demonstrated (1706) p. 521

THE NATURE OF MAN AND GOD

George Fox called men to hearken to God by waiting in stillness, keeping their minds turned to Christ. Thousands of men and women of his day, educated and uneducated, recognized something of God speaking to themselves and found it an adequate source of teaching and strength, not just for everyday life but for extraordinary labours and sufferings.

They appealed to this as a fact of universal experience. Yet it sounds strange today, except to the fairly small numbers involved in the Christian charismatic movement or in the contemplative techniques imported from Eastern religions. Fox would say that we have fallen back into the state from which he called the Christians of his day; the Voice still speaks to us, but like Samuel in the temple we do not know how to name it. Traditional religious language has been devalued, its sincerity tainted, in a number of ways: by being used as an instrument of social control (as Karl Marx indicates) or as an emotional solace (as Freud suggests). So many people are left without a language to describe, even to themselves, widespread and deep experiences.[17]

The first Friends sometimes wrote in language which seems to indicate a level of mystical experience given to very few. 'I am lost in the incomprehensible being of eternal love', writes Francis Howgill.[18] Yet (to continue the analogy of the light) this was like the extreme—invisible to ordinary sight—of a familiar spectrum. Fox talks of a principle in man which responds or answers to that Light, though it may, through disuse and human wilfulness, only catch a few gleams at first. This is the position of most of us. He writes:

> Wait upon God in that which is pure. Though you see little, and know little, and have little, and see your emptiness, and

> see your nakedness, and barrenness, and unfruitfulness, and see the hardness of your hearts, and your own unworthiness; it is the Light that discovers [that is, shows] all this, and the love of God to you, and it is that which is immediate, but the dark understanding cannot comprehend it. So wait upon God in that which is pure, in your measure, and stand still in it every one, to see your Saviour, to make you free from that which the Light doth discover to you [to be evil].[19]

This Light is identified with the Word of John's gospel, 'the true Light, which lighteth every man that cometh into the world', and in following it 'you come to see the state Adam and Eve were in before they fell.'[20]

This account raises a number of difficulties. What is this inner guidance which is supposed to be universal? Is it anything more than that conscience which Freudian psychology explains as the incorporation of parental teaching? Why does Fox refer to the perfectibility of man, a return to the Garden of Eden? It has been said that he seemed to have no personal sense of sin and unworthiness; and since some of his words and actions are open to criticism, he has been accused of smugness or worse. Orthodox Christians may well ask what does he think of the doctrine of Christ's atonement for the sins of the world. Sceptics will want to know how well he understood human nature.

For a time in the nineteenth century, the Society of Friends itself took fright at Fox's reliance on man's direct intuition of the Spirit of God. But psychological insights, a changed view of the Bible, and a better knowledge of other religions, have deepened our understanding and charity towards aspects of the human personality. We can now see that Fox—in his doctrine and in his spells of acute personal distress—points towards something scarcely explored in the traditional concept of sin. It has more in common with those modern theologians who talk of sin as separation. It speaks accurately to many today who can find in their experience no echo of the sentiments of the General Confession of sin. Here, as in the sphere of non-violent political action, George Fox has a message for our time.

He shows himself aware, through his own experience and empathy with others, of the pressures of human instincts and the 'conditions' of human existence. 'The natures of dogs, swine, vipers, of Sodom and Egypt, Pharoah, Cain, Ishmael, Esau, &c . . . I saw within, though people had been looking without. And I cried to the Lord, saying, "Why should I be thus, seeing I was never addicted to commit those evils?" And the Lord answered that it was needful I should have a sense of all conditions, how else should I speak to all conditions . . ?'[21] This imaginative sympathy with the roots of temptation did not imply condoning the evil, but rather partaking in the Light which reveals the evil, judges and destroys it, out of love for struggling man.

Fox has an equal insight into the way in which men deny what they find too painful or demanding, and project their feelings about themselves onto others. Putting a harmless Quaker in gaol is equivalent to imprisoning part of oneself; setting him free is freeing that part. 'Your imprisonments,' he writes, 'will reach to the prisoned [Light] that the persecutor prisons in himself.'[22] Even the man who tries to live 'in the Light' is not free of emotional and moral conflict, though he does have a way to still it; 'for looking down upon sin and corruption and distraction you are swallowed up in it; but looking at the Light that discovers them you will see over them. That will give victory; and you will find grace and strength; and there is the first step of peace.'[23]

What are the elements of this conflict? Fox starts by identifying the same ones as Freud does. There are the pressures of reality, the natural and social world in which we live; for Fox the natural world is wholesome and under the ordering of God, but the social world largely ignores the promptings of the Light. (Freud too raises the question of the 'discontents' of our civilization and the price it exacts from us.) Then there are the demands of our primitive urges and the dictates of the unconscious ('distraction', 'confusion', or 'the darkness' to Fox, 'the id' in Freudian terms).

Next for Freud there is the 'superego', the conscience and awareness of traditional values. It might be expected that Fox would identify this with his source of inward guidance. But he is as aware as any modern psychologist that conscience can be accusing, harassing and destructive, if it is turned in against ourselves. 'Satan's ministers say that the most righteous man that is sins seven times a day; and this both priests and professors have affirmed to my face that it was scripture; but I searched the scriptures and never found any such scripture'.[24] Or a self-satisfied conscience may be the pretext for an attack on others—for Fox (in his own terminology) is as aware as Freud of the aggression of the superego: 'And if people have sinned in their judgement concerning religion, hath Christ bidden you to persecute them for their sins sake? which he died for . . . and the promise is that he will take away their sin.'[25] The Light is not conscience, it is that which can illuminate conscience.

Lastly Freud posits the 'ego', the synthesizing function of the personality, largely conscious, which tries to maintain the balance between the demands of the id, superego and external reality. He would not admit, as a further mental agency or function, the Inward Teacher who does not drive and compel, of whom Fox speaks. Indeed Freud writes: 'It is easy to imagine that certain mystical practices may succeed in upsetting the normal relations between the different regions of the mind, so that, for instance, perception may be able to grasp happenings in the depths of the ego and the id which were otherwise inaccessible to it. It may safely be doubted, however, whether this road will lead us to the ultimate truths from which salvation is to be expected.'[26]

But other psychologists have not been able to limit their views in this way, and bear out a prophecy of T. S. Eliot: 'Psychology . . . can revive, and has to some extent already revived, truths long since known to Christianity, but mostly forgotten and ignored, and it can put them in a form understandable by modern people to whom the language of Christianity is not only dead but indecipherable.'[27]

Whatever it is that Fox is indicating, three of its qualities seem to be important in differentiating it from the ego and superego. In general it has to be sought and drawn on (though it sometimes compels our attention, as Saul discovered on the Damascus road); it gives a sense of tranquillity and certainty; it is both part of us and something more. It is described by William James:

> The individual, so far as he suffers from his wrongness and criticises it, is to that extent consciously beyond it, and in at least possible touch with something higher, if anything higher exists. Along with the wrong part there is thus a better part of him, even though it may be but a most helpless germ. With which part he should identify his real being is by no means obvious at this stage; but when stage two (the stage of solution or salvation) arrives, the man identifies his real being with the germinal higher part of himself; and does so in the following way. He becomes conscious that this higher part is conterminous and continuous with a *more* of the same quality, which is operative in the universe outside of him, and which he can keep in working touch with, and in a fashion get on board of and save himself when all his lower being has gone to pieces in the wreck.[28]

But I can still imagine the reader saying, 'What is this mysterious entity? How does it show itself in my ordinary experience?' We may find one way to answer this question by looking at ethical decisions. It is not hard to realize that moral evaluation is somewhat arbitrary and inadequate, 'founded,' as Jung wrote in the speculations of his old age, 'on the apparent certitudes of a moral code which pretends to know precisely what is good and what evil.'[29] But this realization does not throw most of us into the moral anarchy put forward in the novels of the

Marquis de Sade. Rather than that, we are prepared to accept that the decision on what is right or wrong (as well as which of them to do) is one for which we have to take personal responsibility. 'Once we know how uncertain the foundation is, ethical decision becomes a subjective creative act.' But Jung goes on to say that, though we have lost the guarantee *this is the moral law,* there is something which we find validates our decision. He hesitates whether to call this God (external) or the unconscious (internal), and then decides these terms are equivalent; just as William James identifies the 'higher part' of a man's self with something more 'which is operative in the universe outside of him'. Jung's conclusion about the personal decision on what is right is 'We can convince ourselves of its validity only *Deo concedente*—that is, there must be a spontaneous and decisive impulse on the part of the unconscious.'

A similar insistence on the spirit, which at first may seem wayward and irrational, against the letter of the law and of the scripture, set Fox at odds with the established church of his day. Paul Tillich, a modern theologian well versed in psychology, has described this path in words which could well have been written with George Fox in mind, and which might still describe the Quaker movement at its best today.

> The decisive step to maturity is risking the break away from spiritual infancy with its protective traditions and guiding authorities. Without 'no' to authority, there is no maturity. This 'no' need not be rebellious, arrogant or destructive. As long as it is so, it indicates immaturity by this very attitude. The 'no' that leads to maturity can be, and basically always is, experienced in anxiety, in discouragement, in guilt feelings and despairing inner struggles . . . Much must be left behind: early dreams, poetic imaginations, cherished legends, favoured doctrines, accustomed laws and ritual traditions. Some of them must be restored on a deeper level,

some of them must be given up. Despite this price, maturity can be gained—a manly, self-critical, convincing faith, not produced by reasoning, but reasonable, and at the same time rooted in the message of the divine foolishness, the ultimate source of wisdom.[30]

For the early Friends, the 'decisive impulse of the unconscious' which confirms ethical decision was part of what they understood by Christ, 'the true Light, which lighteth *every man* that cometh into the world.'[31] This quotation from John's gospel has sometimes been called the 'Quakers' text', because they asserted more strongly than most Christians that this illumination was a general and identifiable experience. By 'general' I mean that they believed it came to Mahommedan and American Indian as well as to Christian, to atheist, humanist and agnostic as well as to believer. By 'identifiable' I mean that they gave definite criteria to distinguish it from the disguised gratifications of our unconscious will. Some of these tests have been well stated recently, not in a Quaker context, by the Orthodox priest, Lev Gillett:

> There are very definite criteria to judge guidance. First of all a guidance should not come only once; it must be repeated. Secondly, it must be spoken with the style of God; that is very important. God has his own language, his own style. Grammatically, I should say you can recognize a sentence spoken by God. Thirdly, you may test a guidance by sharing this guidance with other people. Ask four or five people who understand your problem to pray for a solution and to ask for guidance, and see whether the answers are convergent. Fourthly, the most definitive: does this guidance create in you sorrow, bitterness, hatred? Or does it create in you joy and love for God and other people? Judge the tree according to its fruit.[32]

But if one has felt this sense of guidance at times in one's life, it may not seem essential to attach the word 'God' to it. Gillett has also said: 'I am entirely for the elimination of the word "God". The word does not mean anything. It conveys nothing precise or informative or illuminating about Him.'[33] So was it merely arbitrary of George Fox and his friends to identify the guidance they experienced with 'the Holy Spirit' or 'Christ'? Was this just part of the conceptual framework of their day, steeped in the promises of the gospels and *Acts of the Apostles* ('I am the Way, the Truth and the Life')?

I have already suggested that part of our problem here is the lack of a vocabulary we can find meaningful in the way that Fox's vocabulary was meaningful to him and his opponents, even though they fiercely contradicted what he said in it. T. S. Eliot suggests we should draw on the language of psychology; but we must recognize that this mode of description cannot logically claim to be more accurate than Fox's one—it merely offers a different type of explanation. The experiences which have given man a sense of God exist apart from the names we give them or the ways we explain them. Jung acknowledges this rather charmingly in the following discussion:

> Such experiences have a helpful or, it may be, annihilating effect upon man. He cannot grasp, comprehend, dominate them; nor can he free himself or escape from them, and therefore feels them as overpowering. Recognizing that they do not spring from his conscious personality, he calls them mana, daimon or god. Science employs the term 'the unconscious' thus admitting that it knows nothing about it.[34]

Jung goes on to say that the advantage of this term is that it is so banal; it makes no metaphysical claims, and is suited to dispassionate scientific observation. But the religious terms are better at bringing the experiences to life for us and conveying our sense of their meaning.

> Hate and love, fear and reverence enter the scene of the encounter and raise it to a drama . . . The whole man is

challenged and enters the fray with his total reality. Only then can he become whole and only then can 'God be born', that is enter into human reality and associate with man in the form of 'man' . . . in keeping with the saying of Jesus: 'Who sees me, sees the Father'.

This is a hard matter to discuss clearly, because of the difficulties in our understanding of words which are in common use. It is quite common for people to feel that they know what is meant by 'God' and are free to decide whether to believe in 'it' or not. It is less often that one hears them acknowledging that we can only know what is meant by the word through direct experience; though this, in one form, is a leading doctrine of evangelical Christianity. It is very much rarer to hear a Christian concede that another man may have similar experiences to those he calls religious, and allow them to influence his life profoundly and yet be unable to use the word 'God'—so he remains an honest atheist. But this is implied more than once in Jesus' teaching. 'Not everyone that sayeth unto me, Lord, Lord, shall enter into the kingdom of heaven; but he that doeth the will of my Father which is in heaven.'[35]

Another difficulty for us is that early Friends acquired from their background the assumption that the world of matter is sharply divided from that of the spirit, the natural from the supernatural, and the human from the divine. These categories were thought to be exclusive; and this led them to contrast the operation of 'the Light' in them with all human faculties, however noble. That saved them from undue pride in intellect, imagination and other talents. But it also led to an undervaluing of art, literature and philosophy. The white heat of the original Quaker experience induces a sense of profound humility in the face of God's power. But when this declined into a tradition in the second generation, it became a narrowness of spirit which was blind to the spiritual insights expressed in human philosophy, creativity and response to the world of nature.

Fox himself showed his sensitivity to the beauty of literature in his response to the language of the bible, and the blunt nobility of his best writing. Music and art, at the level from which cultured men have drawn some of their deepest spiritual intimations, were almost unknown to him; and architecture spoke to him of the pride and wealth of the great, and the institutional character of organized religion. He was deeply responsive to the living world; its imagery fills his writing. A countryman, he is aware of man's struggle with nature, its extremes, its rhythms, its harshness, as much as its beauty. Men of a pre-scientific, pre-Romantic age, such as Francis of Assisi, Brueghel and Shakespeare, are inclined to see nature as an expression of moral and spiritual truths. Fox did so too, in his own way. I have already quoted the passage in which he says that 'the Creation was opened to me, and it was showed me how all things had their names given them according to their nature and virtue.'* He wanted the study of plants to be included in school curricula, and he once entranced a riding companion with his observations on the language of birds.

In such ways, Fox and his friends do not conform to the 'Puritan image'. They urged the right ordering and understanding of experience, not its denial. Friends were almost alone in their day in feeling their way towards a new mode of thought, in which human and divine could overlap.

In the history of Christian thought, this issue has been focussed on the Incarnation, which is usually seen as a unique event. Friends were trying to understand what had happened to them, but they too saw the incarnation of Christ as a key to explanation. That is to say, they did not use the word 'Christ' because it was conventional to do so—indeed what they said of him put them in danger of trial for blasphemy. They used the word because what they believed about Christ helped them to understand what was happening in their own lives.

* See page 8.

They saw Christ in four aspects. He is the eternal Word of John's gospel, preceding all history. Secondly, he gives substance and meaning to all the prophecies, symbols and leadings towards God of the Jewish religion, and by implication other religious traditions. Thirdly, he is the historical Jesus who, Fox says, wholly embodies these foreshadowings. But lastly, as Fox's friend James Naylor told the magistrates who were examining him on a blasphemy charge in 1652: 'If I cannot witness Christ nearer than Jerusalem, I shall have no benefits by him; but I own no other Christ but that who witnessed a good confession before Pontius Pilate; which Christ I witness in me now.'[36] This is the fourth aspect of Christ, the Light, Spirit or Seed within.

Fox identified this Spirit in man with Jesus Christ (rather than just 'God') because of his initial revelation, 'There is one, even Christ Jesus . . .' and because of Jesus' own words, such as 'Lo, I am with you always, even to the end of the world.'[37] He had read in the Bible that Christ will be known to his people as king and lawgiver, prophet and teacher, shepherd and healer, priest and saviour—the 'offices' or functions of the Light which he too had personally experienced. He is sometimes said to be theologically naive; but his concept of Christ is wonderfully complete. Fox stresses the total adequacy of Christ's relation to each of us in every one of these roles without intermediary. In one or two passages he suggests that man, who is nothing in himself, is prophet, priest and king in so far as he is at one with God. In the same way, when Dante has passed out of Purgatory into Paradise, Virgil says to him, 'Io te sopra te corono e mitrio,' that is, 'I make you king and bishop over yourself.'

But this is not to claim that every man has or can have a total private illumination. Jesus set up a community, and told them to be friends to one another and to him. Fox used the concept of the indwelling Christ not to make unique claims for himself or anyone else, but to emphasize that anyone in the worshipping group, even the child, or the stranger who drops in out of curiosity, may be prompted to say the word which that group (or some person within it) needs to hear. This is what he calls the 'prophetic' word of Christ. This word implies that there is one who knows (Christ) and one who listens (each one of us) and sharply emphasizes his belief that we are talking not about a psychological reality, but an objective one.

George Fox's sanity and humanity are as apparent as his mysticism and sense of mission, in his life and writings. There is no doubt of his religious experience; not a sudden flash, but gradually evolving from his first insight as a troubled and questing young man. His lack of a sense of personal sin and worthlessness is balanced by a keen sensitivity to the evil in the world, both in private lives and political situations; his spiritual participation in what Friends suffered for their witness brought him at times to a state of collapse. I believe that this awareness of external malice was coupled to a sense of danger from within himself. He had known what it is like to contemplate suicide.[38] But, if I am right, he did not repulse and disown this bad part of himself (except perhaps in his controversies with James Naylor and John Perrot, to be mentioned later); rather he faced the task of coming to terms with it. He writes:

> The Lord doth show unto man his thoughts, and discovereth all the secret workings in man. A man may be brought to see his evil thoughts and running mind and vain imaginations, and may strive to keep them down, and to keep his mind in, but cannot overcome them and keep his mind with-in to the Lord. Now in this state and condition, submit to the Spirit of the Lord that shows them, and that will bring to wait upon the Lord and he . . . will destroy them . . . He will discover the root of lusts, and evil thoughts, and vain imaginations, and how they are begotten, conceived and bred, and then how they are brought forth, and how every evil member doth work.[39]

These words surely apply to Fox himself, as well as his readers.

Fox witnesses to the lifelong character of his spiritual struggle in his words as he came out of his last Quaker meeting, a few days before his death: 'I am glad I was here, now I am clear, now I am fully clear.' The nature of this struggle can be seen during the periods of mental stress which I have mentioned (particularly in the years up to 1649, in summer 1658, and in winter 1670–71). His descriptions speak of insecurity and uncertainty, a sense of actual danger, threatening visions, and an almost telepathic identification with the sufferings of others. Some of these descriptions, and an incoherent paper written during one of them, are given at the end of this section. These spells brought physical prostration, sometimes alternating with short bursts of hyperactivity. In each case the period ended with one or more visions which spoke to him of wholeness and integration, and which left him ready to face new problems and demands with deeper spiritual resources. For instance, his almost fatal illness in the winter of 1670 was immediately followed by his strenuous visit to America. 'The conflict between the opposites,' writes Jung, 'can strain our psyche to the breaking point if we take them seriously, or if they take us seriously . . . If all goes well, the solution, seemingly of its own accord, appears out of nature. Then and then only is it convincing. It is felt as "grace". Since the solution proceeds out of the confrontation and clash of opposites, it is usually an unfathomable mixture of conscious and unconscious factors, and therefore a symbol . . .'[40]

Besides these agonising times of reorientation and self-awareness, we may set his penetration into other people, sometimes to depths of which they were unaware. The people of Baycliff said, 'He is such a man as never was, he knows people's thoughts'. He interpreted dreams. Sometimes people could not bear his gaze. He was credited with healing powers. It is not surprising that legends sprang up about him, such as that he could be in different parts of the country at the same time. But there is no doubt from his own and his contemporaries' records that he understood the needs of men, their strengths and weaknesses, and that the practical and mystical went hand in hand with him. The following passage from a paper written in 1650 witnesses to his curiosity and penetration in the area where the spiritual and psychological meet, and shows the imagery he developed to describe this:

> Now some men have the nature of swine wallowing in the mire, and some men have the nature of dogs to bite both the sheep and one another; and some men have the nature of lions, to tear, devour and destroy. And some men have the nature of wolves, to tear and devour the lambs and sheep of Christ; and some men have the nature of the Serpent (that old adversary), to sting, envenom, and poison. 'He that hath an ear to hear, let him hear', and learn these things within himself. And some men have the natures of other beasts and creatures, minding nothing but earthly and visible things, and feeding without the fear of God . . . Thus the evil is but one in all, but worketh many ways; and whatsoever a man's or woman's nature is addicted to, that is outward, the Evil One will fit him with that, and will please his nature and appetite to keep his mind . . . from the Creator.[41]

He did not use this discernment primarily to judge people, but to try to arouse in them the 'witness of God' which would convert (or in his own term, 'convince') them from within. He knew that true change came from the heart; it was not his own words, but that which answered them within the hearer which was meaningful. A priest with whom he had been disputing said—whether ruefully or sarcastically we are not told—'Neighbours, this is the business: George Fox is come to the light of the sun, and now he thinks to put out my starlight'. Fox said, 'Nathaniel, give me thy hand'. Then he told him he would not quench the least measure of God in any, much less put out his starlight if it was true starlight—light from the Morning Star.[42] Kindliness could sometimes call a man to recognize how

God spoke to him; but sternness might be needed. When one man came and told Fox that 'he had had a vision of me: that I was sitting in a great chair, and that he was to come and put off his hat and bow down to the ground before me', Fox said 'Repent, thou beast'.[43] Sometimes a look was enough. A judge, faced with the prospect of having to acquit Fox, decided to catch him after all by ordering him to take the oath of allegiance to the king, knowing he would not swear. 'So I looked him in the face. And the Witness started up in him and made him blush when he looked at me again. For he saw that I saw him.'[44]

Christ is described in the New Testament as the Judge of all mankind. Fox took this to mean that in man's inner experience 'the Light, which comes from Christ Jesus . . . which lets them see and know when they act contrary to it, with this Light they are condemned'.[45] If we are given over to evil, we experience the Light as condemnation—and then we shall be tempted to persecute it when it manifests itself as truth in the life of another man. But if instead we accept the condemnation, we shall then know its healing and saving power.

Can those who reject theological terms make any sense of Fox's account of Christ in us? They will not find an exact correspondence, but I think it is worth noting that two salient and contrasting points in it are picked up in Jung's psychology. These are the surrender to something greater than ourselves which can live through us, and the achievement of spiritual maturity. The following quotations are taken from Anthony Storr's book on Jung:

> Jung calls such an attitude 'religious' although the person who achieves it may not subscribe to any of the recognized creeds. By sacrificing the ego's mundane goals, and accepting what comes, the individual is acknowledging dependence on something beyond the ego, which lives in and through him . . . The attitude of paying careful attention to whatever comes and of acceptance would, I think, be described by religious people as 'waiting upon God'. . .

During his mid-life crisis, as often happens, Jung was forced into a regression in which his childhood problems once more came to the surface. The eventual answer which came to him was the process of individuation. This could be described as a kind of Pilgrim's Progress without a creed, aiming not at heaven, but at integration and wholeness. It was something to live by, and yet it was neither a schizophrenic delusion nor a primitive myth, nor yet an orthodox faith. The end result of the process was becoming an integrated individual, a fully-developed personality in one's own right.[46]

Jung regarded Jesus as someone who had achieved this to an exceptional degree; and his theory of the 'collective unconscious' provides one way of looking at the link between the historical Jesus and the indwelling Spirit. However it should be remembered that, though Jung's views may be based on his own experiences and those of his patients, they go far beyond these observations in their attempts at description and explanation. So do the writings of Paul; so does George Fox. It is important not to deny the truth and relevance of the experience of the Spirit just because we cannot accept the way it is explained. Yet a great deal of religious controversy is on this level.

The psychological attempt to account for these experiences denies that they have any objective validity outside the individual mind. By contrast, the Calvinist doctrine of Jesus' atonement for man's sins seems to place all the emphasis on the saving work of Jesus, while minimising what happens in man's heart. George Fox's claim that the inner Light and the historical Jesus are one builds a delicate bridge between these two viewpoints, enabling each of them to confirm the other. So that when a man experiences the Light teaching, healing and judging him, he can find confirmation that this is no delusion or personal fantasy by turning to the accounts we have of the Jesus of history and finding them consistent with his personal experience. And if they are not consistent . . ? We shall look at this possibility later, when we see how early Friends' beliefs were put to the test historically, in the case of James Naylor.

For this presence which man encounters in the depths of himself, Fox uses an abundance of metaphors: Light, Rock, Ensign, Seed, Anchor, Voice, Hammer, Word, Truth, Life, Lamb, Heavenly Man, Captain, Foundation, and many more. All these are used almost interchangeably with 'Christ Jesus' and 'the Spirit of God'. This has led some to suggest that these last two terms are also metaphor; that Fox was preaching a universalist faith in the truth within the hearts of men, and only the accidents of his time and culture led him to give it a Christian clothing.

It is true that Fox thought his message was universal—because he believed that it was the gospel which Jesus commanded his followers to go into all the world and preach. It was in this conviction that Quakers set out with letters from him to the Great Turk, the Grand Cham of Tartary, Prester John and the Emperor of China. But their content is profoundly Christian, and it would do violence to his thought to suggest that this is somehow accidental. His message could be seen as an amplification and demonstration of Jesus' words: 'I am the Way, the Truth and the Life'.[47] There is a narrow gate to this Way; and Fox thought the gate was so blocked with ritual and observances and dogma and hierarchy that many people had lost the Way. Since he agreed with Paul that the human body was the temple of God, he said we must look into ourselves (and this is the point I have tried to restate with help from modern writers). But he was never in doubt that what we would find there was Christ, teaching and ministering to us in a way consonant with what we read of him in the scriptures.

A Friend recently described how she was drawn, unexpectedly, to this same belief:

The most devastating experience of my religious life was

> the slow discovery, in the bosom of the Society [of Friends], that the 'Spirit', so freely spoken of by Friends, is none other than that mighty Spirit 'who proceeds from the Father and the Son, who, with the Father and the Son together is worshipped and glorified, who spoke by the prophets . . .' The realization grew upon me that I was going to have to face up to this Jesus from whom I had been shrinking, because the Spirit active within me was his witness. I still couldn't even read the gospels, though I knew them fairly well from childhood. I could only *pray to be made ready,* pray that the Spirit would reveal him to me gently so that the shock would not be more than I could bear. So I began praying by instinct, almost in self-defence. For I sensed that the Jesus who was awaiting me was more than the crucified Jesus of history, that in a truly cosmic sense he was Lord.[48]

In his interpretation of Jesus, George Fox seems to go back past the New Testament doctrine of the atonement (which is mainly found in the epistles and John's gospel) to those traditions of Jesus' teaching preserved in the synoptic gospels. There the theme is that the Kingdom of Heaven has now come. It may work unseen as a lump of yeast or a tiny seed; or it may shine out as a precious jewel worth all we own. It may be as hard to find and keep to as a narrow path; or it may come on us as unexpectedly as a burglar. But when it presents itself, a man must grasp it and hold fast; once he has it, everything else he needs will follow. This teaching characterizes the early Quaker experience. But, as we can see in the New Testament, the image of the Kingdom is replaced in early Christian teaching by the image of Christ crucified and risen. Instead of men being urged to seek the Kingdom within and actively co-operate in their own salvation, they are told to believe in the one sufficient sacrifice for the sins of the world; not only is faith in this enough, but nothing else is necessary. I think it would be fair to say that such a formulation awoke no echoes in early Friends' experience, while the gospel of the Kingdom clearly did.

Fox suggests that the events of Jesus' earthly life are in some sense re-enacted within us: the birth of the Light, growth in understanding, baptism and confirmation of God's fatherhood, temptation, the experience of teaching and healing, persecution and mortification, resurrection and ascent into the presence of God. In this way he claims that paradise can be regained, restoring the right relation between man and God, and man and his own will, and male and female, all of which had been distorted by the Fall. It is perhaps significant that we owe the theme of Milton's *Paradise Regained* to another Quaker, Thomas Ellwood, to whom Milton lent the manuscript of *Paradise Lost.* He returned it with the comment, 'Thou hast said much here of paradise lost, but what of paradise found?' Indeed, Fox explicitly demands that we 'must come out of the state that Adam is in, in the Fall, to know the state that he was in before he fell.'[49] No doubt he believed in Adam literally, but to us he reveals the creative potential of the myth:

> It asserts his invincible belief in the perfectibility of all men in God, as stated in the New Testament, but denied in the depressing doctrines of man's depravity and predestination current in his day;
>
> It is the symbol of the state of integration, our lost birthright, restored through the saving action of the inward Christ—and here he quotes with approval from the *Epistle to the Romans,* 'As many as are led by the Spirit of God, they are the sons of God . . . The Spirit itself beareth witness with our spirits that we are the children of God; and if children, then heirs of God, and joint heirs with Christ'[50];
>
> It claims that in this life we can converse with God as Adam did, and partake of eternity. Here we may compare Paul Tillich: 'Eternal life is not a continuation of life after death. Eternal life is beyond past, present and future; we came from it, we live in its presence, we return to it. It is never

absent—it is the divine life in which we are destined to participate in freedom—for God alone has eternity . . . We are mortal, like every creature, mortal with our whole being—body and soul—but we are also kept in the eternal life before we lived on earth, while we are living in time, and after our time has come to an end.'[51]

John Wesley, whose early search had something in common with Fox's, writes this about the state of grace:

> I believe a few, but very few, have an assurance from God of everlasting salvation . . . I believe more have such an assurance of being now in the favour of God as excludes all doubt and fear . . . I believe a consciousness of being in the favour of God (which I do not term . . . full assurance, since it is frequently weakened, nay perhaps interrupted, by returns of doubt and fear) is the common privilege of Christians fearing God and working righteousness. Yet I do not affirm there are no exceptions to this general rule. Possibly some may be in the favour of God, and yet go mourning all the day long.[52]

For most of his life Fox seems to have had this rare 'full assurance'; but he was not alone in this among early Quakers, as passages quoted later in this book will show. One of his favourite scriptures was 'And it shall come to pass afterwards that I will pour out my Spirit upon all flesh; and your sons and your daughters shall prophesy, your old men shall dream dreams, your young men shall see visions; and also upon the servants and the handmaids in those days will I pour out my Spirit.'[53]

And he took seriously the claims of the New Testament that salvation is already come, that our bodies are the temple of God, that if we abide in the Light there is no occasion of stumbling in us.

* * *

What the Light of Christ teaches

Dear Friends, prize your time and the love of the Lord to your souls above all things, and mind that Light in you that shews you sin and evil. Which checks you when ye speak an evil word, and tells you that you should not be proud, nor wanton, nor fashion yourselves like unto the world; for the fashion of this world passeth away. And if ye hearken to that, it will keep you in humbleness of mind, and lowliness of heart, and turn your minds within, to wait upon the Lord, to be guided by it; and bring you to lay aside all sin and evil, and keep you faithful to the Lord; and bring you to wait upon him for teaching, till an entrance thereof be made to your souls, and refreshment come to them from the presence of the Lord. There is your Teacher, the Light, obeying it; there is your condemnation, disobeying it. If ye hearken to the Light in you, it will not suffer you to conform to the evil ways, customs, fashions, delights and vanities of the world; and so lead you to purity, to holiness, to uprightness, even up to the Lord.

Dear hearts, hearken to it, to be guided by it; for if ye love the Light, ye love Christ; if ye hate that, ye hate Christ. Therefore in the name of the Lord Jesus Christ consider of it; and the Lord open your understandings to know him!

G.F.

Epistle 17 (1652) complete.

Give not way to your wills, not busy your selves nor minds with needless or careless words or such things, for they will vail you, and draw your minds from God: but keep within . . . For the Measure is within, and the Light of God is within, and the Pearl is within you which is hid; and the Word of God is within you, and ye are the temples of God, and God hath said he will dwell in you and walk in you.

Epistle 19 (1652)

Yet I was under great temptations sometimes and my inward sufferings were heavy; but I could find none to open my condition to but the Lord alone, unto whom I cried night and day. And I went back into Nottinghamshire, and there the Lord shewed me that the natures of those things which were hurtful without were within, in the hearts and minds of wicked men. The natures of dogs, swine, vipers, of Sodom and Egypt, Pharoah, Cain, Ishmael, Esau, &c., the natures of these I saw within, though people had been looking without. And I cried to the Lord saying, 'Why should I be thus, seeing I was never addicted to commit those evils?' And the Lord answered that it was needful I should have a sense of all conditions, how else should I speak to all conditions; and in this I saw the infinite love of God. I saw also that there was an ocean of darkness and death, but an infinite ocean of light and love, which flowed over the ocean of darkness. And in that also I saw the infinite love of God . . .

Journal (1647) p. 19

The Experience of God's Presence

How may I know that there is a God?

By sinking down into the principle of his own life, wherein he revealeth himself to the creature. There the soul receiveth such tastes and knowledge of him, as cannot be questioned by him that abideth there.

How may a man come to believe in this principle?

In feeling its nature, in waiting to feel somewhat begotten by it, in this its light springs, its life springs, its love springs, its hidden power appears, and its preserving wisdom and goodness is made manifest to the soul that clings to it in the living sense, which its presence and appearance begets in the soul.

How may a man come to obey this principle?

In the faith, in the eyeing of it, in the clinging to it, the strength issues from it into the creature, which maketh [him] able to perform all that it calleth for.

But how may men know that these are true commands of the Lord, and not imaginations or opinions of their own?
When the principle of life is known, and that which God hath begotten felt in the heart, the distinction between what God opens and requires there, and what springs up in man's wisdom, reason and imagination, is very apparent.

Issac Pennington, *Some Questions & Answers Showing Mankind his Duty* (1662)

Baptism and Communion are spiritual realities
Dear Friends, mind the steadfast Guide to the Lord, where we do all meet in the eternal Spirit, in oneness, all being baptised by it into one Body, having one Food, the eternal Bread of Life, which the immortal feed upon, and all made to drink into one Spirit, which is the cup of the communion of the blood of our Lord Jesus Christ, which makes perfect and redeems from all that is earthly, up to God who is holy, pure, spiritual and eternal. And let not any of you in your desires wander from that which is pure in you; then your conditions will be kept clear and pure to see all things as they are, and a clear separation will be made from that which is of man and of your own, and that which is of God; and there will be a growing up in that which is pure. And so, be low in your minds, waiting for the coming of our Lord Jesus Christ in you all, who is Lord over all, to be Lord over all in you. And so the Lord God of Power keep you all! Farewell.

G.F.

Epistle 31 (1653) complete.

Original sin is to be laid at man's door, not God's
As for the soul, that is immortal, for God breathed into man the breath of life and made man a living soul, and sin came by disobedience—and that separates between man and God who is pure and hath all souls in his hand; but as for you who are in a cave of darkness, the mystery of the soul is from you hidden, but

you confess it is by your means that sin is conveyed to your children. Yea, take it to yourselves, it is your work and the Lord hath no hand in it, not in sin nor in making sinners.

The Great Mistery (1659) p. 363

[Richard Baxter] saith, Christ's kingdom is a hospital, and has no subjects in it but diseased ones.

Answer: We read of no such thing in scripture, that Christ's kingdom is a hospital, and his subjects are diseased ones. But they who follow the Lamb, in their mouth is no guile, nor spot, nor fault before the throne of God . . .; and they are the faithful, and called, and chosen that overcome the world, and his kingdom stands in power and in righteousness and joy in the Holy Ghost, and is not a 'hospital', nor his subjects diseased ones, for he heals them, and converts them, and washes them. The diseased, or such as come to Christ to be healed, them who come to him he heals them of what infirmity soever it be, and cures them, and clothes them in the right mind.

The Great Mistery (1659) p. 30

In a time of persecution

As I had a time to preach the Truth amongst you, to the convincement of many, so also now I have a time to seal the same with patient suffering in the bonds of the gospel, that you may see that it is no other but what we are made able and willing to seal with patient suffering, yea, with our blood, if we be called to it . . .

I charge you all in the name of the God of Truth, be faithful, valiant and bold for the Truth received: and as you have received it, so walk in it: that you may profess no more in word but what in life you feel; that the Light may be preached both in your lives and shine forth in your conversation. And be willing that self shall suffer for the Truth, and not the Truth for self.

James Parnell, *Letter to Friends in Essex* (1656)
written from Chelmsford gaol, where he died of
starvation and exposure, aged eighteen.

And there I lay at the widow Dry's all that winter, warring with the evil spirits, and could not endure the smell of any flesh meat.

And I saw all the religions and people that lived in them, and the priests that held them up, as a company of man-eaters, and how they ate up the people like bread, gnawing the flesh off their bones. And great sufferings was I under at this time beyond words to declare, for I was come unto the deep, and the man-eaters were about me and I warred with their spirits.

And at this time there were great persecutions and there had been searching for me at London, and some meeting-houses plucked down and broken up with soldiers. Sometimes they would come with a troop of horse and a company of foot, and they would break their swords and muskets, carbines and pikes, with beating Friends and wounding [in] abundance, so that the blood stood like puddles in the streets. And Friends were made to stand, by the Lord's power . . . And it was a cruel bloody persecuting time, but the Lord's power went over all, and his everlasting Seed. And as persecution began to cease, I began to arise out of my sufferings.

As for religion and worship and ministers of God, alack! I saw there was none in the world amongst those that pretended it, but amongst such as were in the Truth. I saw the church as a company of man-eaters of cruel visages and of long teeth. Though they had cried against the men-eaters of New England, I saw they were in the same natures . . .

So in my deep misery I saw things beyond words to utter; and I saw a black coffin but I passed over it.

And at last I overcame these spirits and men-eaters though many times I was so weak that people knew not whether I was in the body or out.

Journal (1670) p. 571

Visions at the time of his distress of mind

Many things more did I see concerning the heavenly city, the new Jerusalem, which are hard to be uttered . . .

Oh, this blessed city is appeared. Oh, glorious things will come to pass. You will see glorious things will come. I desire, I wish, that these outward powers of the earth were given up. I can tell what to say to them. Oh, hypocrisy! It makes me sick to think of them. I have given them a visitation and as faithful a warning as ever was. There is an ugly a slubbering hound, an ugly hound, an ugly slubbering hound. But the Lord forgive them—destruction, destruction. We have given them indeed a visitation and salutation and they will not hear, but refuse it and reject the Lord. But we shall be clear of all their blood.

Journal (1671) p. 575

A dream at the end of this period of inward suffering

And I had a vision about the time that I was in this travail and sufferings, that I was walking in the fields and many Friends were with me, and I bid them dig in the earth, and they did and I went down. And there was a mighty vault top-full of people kept under the earth, rocks and stones. So I bid them break open the earth and let all the people out, and they did, and all the people came forth to liberty; and it was a mighty place. And when they had done I went on and bid them dig again. They did, and there was a mighty vault full of people, and I bid them throw it down and let all the people out, and so they did.

And I went on again, and bid them dig again, and Friends said unto me, 'George, thou finds out all things', so there they digged, and I went down, and went along the vault; and there sat a woman in white looking at time how it passed away. And there followed me a woman down in the vault, in which vault was the treasure; and so she laid her hand on the treasure on my left hand and then time whisked on apace; but I clapped my hand upon her and said 'Touch not the treasure.' And then time passed not so swift.

They that can read these things must have the earthy, stony nature off them. And see how the stones and the earth came upon man since the beginning, since he fell from the image of God and righteousness and holiness. And much could I speak of these things, but I leave them to the right eye and reader to see and read.

Journal (1671) p. 578

The Nature of Christ

And there is no true Witness within but the Light, the Life and Spirit of Christ, the true Record; no true faith but that which Christ is the author of, which giveth victory; no true Anchor to the immortal soul but by Christ, the Hope of glory (so by Hope you are saved); no true liberty but in Christ, and in his law of the Spirit of Life, and in his gospel; no true knowledge of God but by his Light and Spirit in the heart; no salvation but by the name of Jesus; no true praying but in the Spirit, no true singing but in the Spirit; no true Foundation but Christ, to build upon; no true fast but that which breaks the bond of iniquity; no true fellowship but in the pure faith, Light, Spirit and gospel of God and Christ; no true foundation but Christ, to build upon; no true Way but Christ; no true Seed but what Christ hath sown in the heart; no true rest but in Christ; no true service to God and Christ but in the newness of life; no knowing the things of God but by the Spirit of God; no knowing the Son nor the Father but by the revelation of the Holy Spirit; no knowing the scriptures but by the same Holy Ghost that moved the holy men to give them forth; no calling Jesus 'Lord' but by the Holy Ghost by which he was conceived; no grafting into Christ but by believing in the Light, which is called 'the Light' in men and 'the Life' in him; no true wisdom but from above; and no true receiving it but in the fear of the Lord; and no true understanding of spiritual things but what Christ gives; no Divine Reason but in the faith that Christ is the author of, which giveth victory over that which is unreasonable and separates from God; and no true love to God but what he sheddeth abroad in the heart. And to know a fellowship with Christ in his death and sufferings is above the fellowship of bread and wine, which will have an end; but the fellowship in the gospel and Holy Spirit hath no end.

Epistle 230 (1663)

On his travels in America at the age of fifty

The great Lord God of heaven and earth and creator of all, who is over all, carried us by his high hand and mighty Power and Wisdom over all, and through many dangers and perils by sea and land . . . and perils of wolves, bears tigers and lions; and perils of rattlesnakes and other venomous beasts of like poisonous nature; and perils through great swamps, and bogs, and the wilderness, where no way was but for such-like creatures, where we travelled and lodged in the night by fires; and perils over great bays, creeks and rivers, in open small boats and small canoes; and perils in great storms and tempests in the ocean, which many times were beyond words to utter; and great perils through the Indian countries in the woods or wildernesses by man-eaters, some whereof lay in wait for some of our company that passed from us, but they were discovered, for the Lord's power gave them dominion over all; and great perils by night through the cold, rain, frosts, snow, in lying in the woods and wilderness several nights together until some of our company had their hands and fingers benumbed, (whereas some of the world at such times have had some their noses and some their fingers and toes frozen off—I was an eye-witness of some of these things); and perils of robbers by land and pirates by sea, these troublesome times, whereof the sea abounds.

The blessed Lord God, in his blessed Power, who by his Power stretched over all these workers of death his line of life, the Lord God made all easy by his Spirit and Power, and gave his people dominion over all and made all plain and low as a meadow, and made his great Power and Glory in his Light and Truth known over all in the hearts of people, blessed be his name for ever, Amen.

Journal (1673) p. 661

On the voyage home from America, when the ship's crew and passengers feared pirates

The Lord God said, 'Into thy hand and power I have given thee the ship and all that is in it,' that it should come safe, and Paul's words came into my mind. And I told the company I believed in God. And when we came near home the Lord God said to me, after he had given the ship into my hand, 'Canst thou give up thy self, ship and all that is in it now, to be taken by the pirates so that all the ships that are behind in Virginia and Maryland might come safe to England?' And I freely did it. And in the twinkling of an eye it was given back to me again, and the blessed God brought us well and safe home.

Journal (1673) p. 663

Eternity

Friends, meet together and know one another in that which is eternal, which was before the world was.

Epistle 149 (1657)

He that inhabits eternity dwells with an humble heart.

Epistle 364 (1680)

All is well. The Seed of God reigns over all, and over death itself. And though I am weak in body, yet the Power of God is over all, and the Seed reigns over all disorderly spirits.

From among his dying words, reported in Thomas Ellwood's edition of the *Journal.*

TRIAL AND SETBACK

'Let me show you,' thundered Dr Hickes in a sermon to the University of Oxford in 1680, 'what a dangerous, damnable and precarious principle that is which asserts that immediate revelation or inspiration is not ceased, but is a standing and perpetual gift in the Church of Christ.'[54] And indeed the Quaker attitude towards sin and perfection had its dangers. Was the vision of the individual paramount? Was there to be no external authority? In that case, as its enemies pointed out, there was no fundamental difference between them and the Ranters, who were not an organized group but a loose movement concerned with radical thought. They spread their ideas by becoming wandering speakers, and the torrent of pamphlets on religious matters which poured from the presses during the Commonwealth owed much to them. Some of them were deeply exercised about the paradoxes of good and evil, God and nature; others simply enjoyed the advantages of a philosophy which devalued all ethical codes . . . 'the merriest of all devils for extempore lascivious songs, . . . for healths, music, downright bawdry and dancing'.[55]

The historian Christopher Hill suggests that the Quaker movement up to 1659 'was far closer to the Ranters in spirit than its leaders later liked to recall, after they had spent many weary hours differentiating themselves from Ranters and ex-Ranters.'[55] One of the best known seventeenth-century Friends, William Penn, looking backward from 1692, identified a number of Quakers in the earliest days who 'would have every man independent, that as he had the Principle in himself, he should only stand and fall to that, and nobody else; and though the measure of Light and Grace might differ, yet the nature of it was the same; and being so, they struck at the spiritual unity which a people guided by the same Principle are naturally led into.'[56] The potential tension between this independent principle and this spiritual unity convulsed the Quaker movement three times during the lifetime of George Fox; and in the first of these, the controversy over James Naylor, the doctrine of the Inward Light was severely tested. To understand this, we must return to the events of Fox's life.

How did it come about that George Fox's solitary mission first became a movement? After his first religious experiences and early imprisonments, he spent some time in the Midlands, and groups of Friends began to form. Then he turned northwards to areas largely neglected by the established churches. There he found groups of 'seekers' already meeting, often with an earnest religious sense to which his message gave coherent expression. Francis Howgill, one of them, writes:

> We were reckoned, in the North of England, even as the outcasts of Israel, and as men destitute of the great knowledge which some seemed to enjoy; and yet there was more sincerity and true love amongst us and desires after the living God than was among many who ran into heaps and forms but left the cross behind them . . . And God, out of his great love and great mercy, sent one to us, a man of God, one of ten thousand, to instruct us in the way of God more perfectly . . .'[57]

The 'first publishers of Truth', the original preachers of the Quaker message, were mainly yeomen and craftsmen from the north, including Howgill, Naylor and William Dewsbury, all of whom describe in their writings spiritual experiences before the arrival of Fox. To the scandal of some contemporaries, a number of these preachers were women. The movement found some support among the gentry, justices and clergy in those parts, though such people might be alienated by Friends' individualism and their refusal to pay tithes to the church. Sometimes there was opposition so extreme that one suspects the persecutor was deeply touched by their teaching and violently repudiated his own feelings. Fox was imprisoned in Carlisle in 1653. But a letter from Parliament released him, and his gaoler was imprisoned in his place.

A mission to the south of England was set on foot the following year; the Quakers were now a movement, preparing their way with pamphlets, advance parties who sent back reports, and visits to Cromwell himself. Now that they were an identifiable group they were met with more suspicion. Their avowed intention was not to form a sect, but to bring the whole world back to true religion. This claim awoke the anti-Catholic feeling which was never far away in seventeenth-century England; and in spite of their theology they were accused of being Jesuits in disguise, working for a political takeover. Their non-violent principles were not fully formulated, and would not have been trusted in any case. It was not easy to distinguish between the different groups forming at the time, more or less fanatical: 'Quakerism is become the common sink of them all,' said one of its opponents. In a time of such uncertainty and so many challenges to conventional beliefs, it is no wonder that the establishment became alarmed and hoped to strike a mortal blow at the leadership of the group which they identified as the most vigorous.

But there was no single human leadership, only God. The early Quaker evangelists (and their successors down to today) travelled as they felt led by the Spirit. They corresponded to encourage one another, not to command. In January 1656, George Fox was imprisoned in Launceston, Cornwall; and many of the other missionaries were also in prison, or back in the north and midlands, or in Ireland. But James Naylor, considered by many contemporaries to be their most notable preacher, was in London, under great pressure from would-be followers and with little solid support. An over-enthusiastic atmosphere developed in which he was paid exaggerated honours; one man was to write to him, 'Thy name shall be no more James Naylor, but Jesus'. He said later that fear struck him when he received this, and he put it in his pocket, intending no-one to see it, as he could not own to the contents. However he did not reprove the sender. A woman claimed that he had raised her from the dead. Over the distance that separated them, tensions arose between Naylor, strained to the point of exhaustion, and Fox, isolated and ill-treated in prison. Each misjudged the other. Other Friends were urging Fox to publish a statement condemning Naylor, afraid he had already hesitated too long. When they did meet, they quarrelled; and when Naylor would have kissed Fox, Fox offered him his foot to kiss.

The issue caused passionate debate at the time, which has been revived in our own day. Beneath the personal conflict lay a fundamental issue: was the Guidance within which was claimed by the individual infallible? Fox could see in Naylor (more clearly perhaps than in himself) the possibility of unchecked individuality diverging from the divine illumination in which he believed. Other Friends expected him to settle the issue by his personal authority. In the unity so often felt at the start of a great venture, they had not yet needed to discover ways of reconciling different perceptions of the Truth. Naylor's excitable women followers were openly and bitterly critical of Fox, yet Naylor refused to restrain them at Fox's request.

Naylor's excuse for not doing so, given later, was that he did not wish to quench whatever was 'of God' in what they said and did. It has generally been assumed that at the time he did not have the emotional strength to withstand their influence, and this is borne out by contemporary descriptions of his passive, exhausted demeanour. However he was still justifying his behaviour by appealing to divine guidance, and so implicitly challenging Fox's spiritual insight. Fox did repudiate some of Naylor's followers: 'Martha Simmonds and Stranger and his wife is denied for their lies and slanders & so judged out with the Truth.'[58] Whether he would eventually have done the same to Naylor, or whether the Spirit would have shown a way of reconciliation was never known; events now took an unexpected direction.

On 24th October, 1656, James Naylor rode into Bristol in pouring rain, and his followers strewed garments in his way and sang 'Holy, holy, holy', as a symbol of the second coming of Christ, which many looked for in those days, and which Quakers believed had taken place—spiritually—in them. The city authorities at once arrested him. The letter paying him divine honours was found in his pocket. This gave Parliament the opportunity to discredit Quakers by arraigning him for blasphemy. It is a measure of the importance they attached to this matter that the debate lasted three weeks. Naylor's defence was still to claim direct guidance.

> I do abhor that any honour due to God should be given to me as I am a creature. But it pleased the Lord to set me up as a sign of the coming of the Righteous One. And what has been done as I passed through the towns, I was commanded by the Lord to suffer such things to be done by me, as to the outward, as a sign, not as I am a creature [that is, usurping the honour due to the Creator].[59]

Parliament illegally sentenced him to be whipped, branded, bored through the tongue, humiliated and imprisoned. He underwent these punishments with heroic patience, after embracing the executioner. His name, and the word 'Quaker', were suddenly notorious through Europe. We can trace in pamphlets and private letters how the other leading Quakers tried to dissociate themselves from his extravagances and the taint of blasphemy, though several of them visited him in prison. William Dewsbury, one of the wisest and most loveable of them, encouraged him to write letters expressing his sorrow that he had brought shame and suffering on Friends, and condemning the spirit of enmity which his actions—or failure to act—had encouraged. Naylor now disclaimed the divine Leading which he had earlier justified himself by: 'I reasoned against God's tender reproof . . . and his pure Spirit was grieved, and he ceased to reprove, and he gave me up, and his Light he withdrew and his Judgement took away.'[60] This undermined any opposition which might be using his name within the Quaker movement, reaffirming the unity of the Spirit by which Quakers claimed to be guided. It also answered the propaganda of their enemies: 'J.N. and G.F. at daggers drawn discovers their cheat of both being led by an infallible Spirit.'[61]

In 1658 he was released from prison, and went to see George Fox. Fox was ill at the time, in one of the periods of anguish which I have described; and Naylor was rebuffed, as he tells in the letter quoted on page 76. Next year William Dewsbury brought them together, only a few months before Naylor's death. 'Mighty was the Lord's majesty,' writes Dewsbury, 'amongst his people in the day he healed up the breach which had been so long to the sadness of the hearts of many. The Lord clothed my dear brethren Geo.Fox, Edward Burrough, Fras. Howgill, with a precious wisdom. A healing Spirit did abound within them with the rest of the Lord's people there that day . . . and dear James Naylor, the Lord was with him.'[62] It is notable too how hesitant and even incoherent Fox's Journal becomes as it approaches the last months of 1659, and how its vigour and power revive after the date of his meeting with his old comrade;[63] though it is a disappointment that he does not describe the reconciliation. (The Journal was dictated many years after the events it recounts.)

So it would be possible to see in this episode no more than an incipient breach which was averted. But I have told it at some length because it touches on lasting issues. Early Friends believed that one of the 'offices' of Christ is judgement. Thus Fox could assert that he did not judge Naylor himself but 'set the Power of God over him'. Naylor in his turn could say that he felt this inward judgment while he was in prison and it saved him. But if disputes arose in future, and neither party would admit to being in error, the Naylor affair gave no indication of a way forward. It did however show that the Quaker movement was not so vulnerable as its enemies had hoped.

From a practical point of view, Fox deserved the support which the great majority of Friends had offered him. But in condemning his friend for 'running out into imaginations', Fox may have allowed the authoritarian and practical side of his own nature to condemn the more spontaneous and visionary aspects. These events brought inevitable and necessary lessons to those involved in them, and ensured the survival of the Quakers; but they also mark the beginning of a shift from unlimited vision and self-sacrifice to the arts of caution necessary for that survival. It was not long before the sober, respectable Quaker image began to replace that of the wandering enthusiast with his revelations from God and revolutionary zeal. Men such as William Penn, son of an admiral, wealthy, a friend of James II, and Isaac Penington, son of a Lord Mayor of London, and Robert Barclay, son of a Scottish laird and trained in theology, joined or came to prominence. It may be that their church could only survive in this way, by establishing itself as an institution. But some Friends today feel that their Society never recaptured the qualities which were symbolically cast out with James Naylor. Looking at its subsequent history, through a period of withdrawal from the world, commercial success, enlightened social witness, the evangelical movement, to the 'Quakerism' of today, one may feel it owes almost as much to the sober rationalism of the contemporary John Locke, as to the mysticism and prophetic fire of the early Fox and Naylor.

The leading Friends of the first generation were great pamphleteers, and when they died it was customary to publish a 'Collected Works'. In James Naylor's case this did not appear until nearly fifty years after his death. In its pages he qualifies the Quaker doctrine of human perfectibility in the Light by his sharp awareness of the ebb and flow of spiritual strength, the possibility of self-deception, and our need to understand the shadow side of our personality. He writes of how he experienced judgement and mercy as one, how he was able to lay aside all resentments and find peace, love and strength in the utter loss of himself. Quakers have from time to time recaptured this in their own experiences, but one can only regret that it was not more firmly incorporated in their main tradition.

George Fox has been described as a very 'masculine' personality, using the word in favourable and unfavourable senses. And it has been suggested that James Naylor complemented him with a more 'feminine' temperament. I am not sure that there is much value in attempting to label these two men with stereotypes which are beginning to lose their meaning for us, and which do not correspond to the ways in which people thought about personality in their own day. I have drawn attention to intuitive, tender and responsive elements in Fox's make-up. We know nothing of his sexual life, and nothing out of the ordinary about his views on the sexual relationship; but we know that in practice he lived up to his views on the equality and partnership of men and women. Private letters and snatches of reported conversation as well as public testimonies, witness to the quality of his personal relationships.

Anxiety for the fragile community of Friends precipitated Fox's response to Naylor, and later John Perrot. One may feel, sadly, but with understanding, that in this anxiety he did not trust enough to the power of the Spirit to preserve its own—and as a consequence he unconsciously revealed a rejecting, authoritarian side of himself. This need not surprise us; but what we must ask is whether he allowed this, (as so many religious leaders have done) to be the first step on the road to spiritual dictatorship, or whether the Light found a way (as he claimed it could) to redeem this shadow in himself.

Amongst Friends today, one sometimes feels that there is not enough awareness of the darkness in the human personality; instead, a denial of aggression (for instance in the way they sometimes present their testimony against war) and an excess of light and sweetness. Even the original editors of Fox, Naylor and later John Woolman, sometimes felt obliged to suppress their accounts of miracles, denunciations, conflicts, dreams and nightmares, and so contributed an incomplete account of their experience.* Such editing tends to destroy what it is trying to preserve, because it leads away from a mature grasp of experience with its heights and depths, into the wishful thinking of 'everything is for the best in this best of all possible worlds'. Such a facile philosophy bearing their names is an injustice to Fox and Naylor, who in their different ways endured terrifying struggles with the evil in themselves and in the world; it also deprives their message of much value for the modern seeker after Truth.

Two years after Naylor's death, another controversy arose, excited by a Quaker called John Perrot. He had attempted to preach in Rome, and suffered three years' imprisonment in a madhouse by order of the Inquisition. He raised the question of whether 'customary, traditional ways of worship' were already creeping in among Friends. The practices complained of were slight; most prominent in the controversy was that of taking off one's hat while praying in a Quaker meeting. To Fox, this was a matter of turning Friends from unity in the power of God into vain and useless disputes. He wrote a letter of disownment and condemnation which was read to Perrot on shipboard, about to leave for Barbados. In this way Fox exercised the authority which many Friends expected from him; but feelings were running strongly enough on both sides for this to raise again the danger of splitting the movement in two. It was not Fox but Dewsbury who spoke, in a letter to Perrot which he published, of the need for reconciliation, and of God's power to preserve his own Truth.

> And as to my particular [self], it is not my nature to be found striving with thee or any upon the earth; but, having declared the Truth to thee, I will return to my rest in the Lord, and let every birth live the length of its day; and let

* A friend advised me to omit the extract on pp. 58–9 because it 'makes Fox look ridiculous'.

time manifest what is born of God, for that spirit that stands up in self-striving will weary itself and die, and end in the earth.[64]

Thus Quakers, like every revolutionary movement, had to face the question of internal authority. George Fox's natural authority, both by temperament and as founder, was liable to take the course already charted in the case of Perrot. This was probably reinforced by the anxieties and loyalties of a great many Friends, and by the deaths, at about this time, of quite a number of 'the first publishers of Truth', Fox's original co-workers. But from 1664 to 1666 Fox endured a harrowing imprisonment at Lancaster and Scarborough: 'My body was numbed with cold, and my fingers swelled, that one was grown as big as two.'[65] During this time, the question of authority was still an urgent one; and in his absence, a specially convened meeting issued a letter committing a power of decision and judgement to 'such good ancient Friends as have been and are sound in the Faith, and agreeable to the witness of God in his people.'[66] The reaction to the dangers of individual guidance was creating the beginnings of a hierarchy, of which Fox could have expected to be the pinnacle.

But when he was released, he had a new vision, of a structure for Friends without human leadership, where balance could be achieved between the insight of the individual and the corporate wisdom of his own group of Friends. To achieve this, Fox revived the 'monthly meetings' which had existed in some places during the Commonwealth but had often disappeared during the more recent persecutions. Ill as he was, he rode round the country establishing a complete system of these meetings. The Monthly Meeting is formed of the members of the ordinary meetings which comprise it; any or all of them can attend. In business affairs, as in all other matters, the decider is the Spirit of God, known in the hearts of those present. No decision will be made until each of them thinks it is acceptable. Matters of concern are referred to Monthly Meeting from the constituent meetings; and each Monthly Meeting can refer them to the Yearly Meeting which can take action on behalf of the whole Society of Friends in the country.

Fox's further travels in Britain were in support of this autonomous system, so well suited to Friends' understanding of the Spirit that he was justified in calling it 'gospel order'. His presence and his letters must have carried much weight; yet we sometimes read of him leaving most of the speaking to his companions and playing little active part. He wrote: 'The least member in the Church hath an office and is serviceable, and every member hath need one of another.'[67] The extent to which he surrendered his leading position was one of the most remarkable things in his life. Though he is seldom explicit about the struggles of his own conscience, I think we may see in this the outcome of a long process of self examination and readjustment, in the light of the events I have described and the promptings of the Spirit he encountered within himself.

* * *

Victory over temptation and suffering

And Friends, though you may have tasted of the power and been convinced and have felt the light, yet afterwards you may feel winter storms, tempests and hail, and be frozen, in frost and cold and a wilderness and temptations. Be patient and still in the Power and still in the Light that doth convince you, to keep your minds to God; in that be quiet, that you may come to the summer, that your flight be not in the winter time. For if you sit still in the patience which overcomes in the power of God, there will be no flying. For the husbandman, after he hath sown his seed, he is patient. For by the Power and by the Light you will come to see through and feel over winter storms, tempests, and all the coldness, barrenness, emptiness. And the same Light and Power will go over the Tempter's head, which Power and Light were before he was. And so in the Light standing still you will see your salvation, you will see the Lord's strength, you will feel the small rain, you will feel the fresh springs in the Power and Light, your minds being kept low . . . You will see God revealing his secrets, inspiring, and his gifts coming unto you, through which your hearts will be filled with God's love; praise be to him which lives for evermore, in which Light and Power his blessings are received. And so the eternal Power of the Lord Jesus Christ preserve and keep you in that.

Journal (1656) pp. 283–4

Enduring persecution cheerfully

And I was moved to write to those justices and to tell did we ever resist them when they took our ploughs and plough-gear, our cows and horses, our corn and cattle, and kettles and platters from us, and whipped us and set us in the stocks, and cast us in prison, and all this for serving and worshipping of God in spirit and truth and because we could not conform to their religions, manners, customs and fashions. Did we ever resist them? Did we not give them our backs and our cheeks and our faces to spit on, and our hair to pluck at? . . . And they thought to have ruined and undone us, but they ruined themselves. But we could praise God, notwithstanding all their plundering of us, that we had a kettle, and a platter, and a horse and plough still . . . But our backs and cheeks were ready . . . and we could and can turn them to all the smiters on the earth; and we did not look for any help from men, but our helper was and is the Lord.

Journal (1661) p. 406

There came one of his servants with a naked sword and run at me ere I was aware of him, and set it to my side and there held it, and I looked up at him in his face and said to him, 'Alack for thee, it's no more to me than a straw.'

Journal (1649) p. 49

Experience under torture

It is also very memorable to me how wonderfully the Lord, by his divine Power, supported me, even at that very instant while they were inflicting their cruelty . . . that even then my spirit was raised and my mouth opened to sing aloud in praises to the Lord my God, that he counted me worthy to suffer for his name and truth-sake.

George Whitehead, *Christian Progress* (1725) p. 35.

Advice in times of controversy

Go not forth to the aggravating part, to strive with it without the Power of God, lest you hurt yourselves, and run into the same nature, out of the Life. For patience must get the victory and answer that of God in every one, must bring every one to it, and bring them from the contrary.

So let your moderation, and temperance, and patience be known to all men in the Seed of God. For that which reacheth to the aggravating part of man without Life sets up the aggravating part, and breeds confusion, and hath a life in outward strife, and reacheth not to the witness of God in every one, in which they come into peace and covenant with God, and fellowship with another.

Letter to Friends during the controversy over James Naylor, *Journal* (1656) p. 281.

On the contention surrounding James Naylor

And as concerning this thing, which was looked upon as a breech among us by many, yet it's over, and Truth stands a-top of it, and the beauty of Truth appears through it all, and Truth is more lovely when it is proved and purged.

Edward Burrough in the Preface to *The Cause of Stumbling Removed* by Richard Hubberthorne (1657)

Dearly beloved Sister,

Thou art often in my remembrance, and my heart is to see thee when God wills; in whose counsel and Life I desire to walk, to his praise alone, who hath thus far redeemed me out of deep adversity; and doth still work with me and for me (as I abide in his patience and obedience) making my way through many oppositions and trials. In his will alone I desire to rest and be still; who in the needful time hath still appeared—praises be to him for ever!

I suppose thou may have heard of my going to see our beloved G.F. at Reading, which in tenderness of love I did, as soon as I was got out of prison, hearing he was not well: but I was not permitted to come where he was; which my enemy rejoiced at, that thereby he might add sorrow to affliction:—but my spirit was quieted, in that simplicity in which I went, in that to return: and gave me his Peace therein, as though I had had my desire—blessed be the Lord God of my mercy for this thing; who still becomes my Peace, and his presence is with me in what he moved me to, which is my comfort and refreshment—and so his will is my peace.

James Naylor in a letter to Margaret Fell, Summer 1658

Overcoming by suffering

And this Seed all should know, which is beloved by the Father and Heir of the everlasting kingdom, who strives not by violence but entreats; who seeks not revenge but endures all contradictions from all against himself, to the end he may obtain mercy for all from the Father. And this is the Seed of eternal Peace, and the eternal Peacemaker, which was fore-ordained of the Father, and hath power to endure all things, and subdue all things by overcoming.

So seek this in yourselves and all men, and in it seek one another as brethren. This is that which is perfect and is never to be done away, neither can it be overcome of the world. Wrath cannot enter it, pride cannot enter it. It strives for nothing but to live its own life, which the world strives not for; nor can any that are of it strive with it. The worldly spirit seeks not that crown whose life is to suffer all things, to be meek, and low, and poor, and rejected; reviled, contemned of all the world, bearing the reproach of all that's above* that of God in all. And little striving in the will of man is there for this kingdom, or the cross that belongs thereto, which no exalted* mind can bear or glory in.

James Naylor, *Epistle XI.*
Written during or soon after his time in prison.

We, in love to our brethren that lie in prisons and houses of correction and dungeons, and many in fetters and irons, and have been cruelly beat by the cruel gaolers, and many have been persecuted to death, and have died in prison, and many lie sick and weak in prison and on straw, so we, in love to our brethren, do offer up our bodies and selves to you, for to put us as lambs into the same dungeons and houses of correction, and their straw and nasty holes and prisons; and do stand ready a sacrifice for to go into their places in love to our brethren, that they may go forth, and that they may not die in prison as many of the brethren are dead already. For we are willing to lay down our lives for our brethren, and to take their sufferings upon us that you would inflict upon them. And if our brethren suffer we cannot but feel it, and Christ saith it is he that suffereth and was not visited . . .

We whose names are hereunto subscribed, being a sufficient number to answer for the present sufferers, are waiting in Westminster Hall for an answer from you to us . . .

A Paper signed by 164 Friends and sent
into Parliament in 1659

During imprisonment in Scarborough Castle
I have been uncapable to write or receive writing for a long time,

* Above, exalted: in the negative sense of 'too proud', 'too lofty'.

or to speak, or bear to be spoken to, but have been as a man buried alive; for else I should have writ to you before now. And therefore, O dear friends, give no occasion of stumbling; keep tender, for hardness of heart is worse than an outward plague—for that brings destruction many ways—and so grieve not the Spirit in others, nor in yourselves. And whatsoever is decent and comely, follow; honest and of good report, that makes for peace and not for strife under pretence of love (for that's not of God). For God, who is Love, is not the author of strife and confusion, but of Peace.

Epistle 244 (1666)

Tenderness to those who are seeking Truth

No man after he hath beaten his child hateth him ever afterwards, but loveth him (if he repent and amend so doth the eternal Father), and if the child be fallen down into the dirt, he doth not go and tumble him more into the dirt, or into the ditch, and there let him lie in the dirt and ditch, but takes him out and washes him; and so doth the heavenly Father which leads his children by his hand and dandles them upon his knee. And so all that be called fathers in the Truth, or mothers, their tenderness should be the same to all little children in the Truth that can hardly go without leading, that sometimes may fall into the dirt and ditch, and slip aside, and then be troubled and cry. To such there should be tenderness shown and to wash them, and help them, and love to such should be manifest, for there is a difference betwixt a stubborn rebellious and wilful child and one that is penitent . . .

Epistle 262 (1668)

God's faithfulness

Whom God loves, he loves to the end; where the eternal unity is there is all peace, all clean, no jar, who are all of one mind, hid from the world's wisdom, knowledge, comprehension and thoughts, which can never enter it.

Gospel Truth Demonstrated (1706) p. 3

THE WORSHIPPING COMMUNITY

The public witness which Friends have borne for peace, for the equality of men and women, for fair prices and for other beliefs and aspirations, is called—in Quaker parlance—'the testimonies'. In modern Quaker thinking, such activity is sometimes contrasted with worship and spiritual search. But for George Fox, the way of silent worship was the fundamental testimony. 'Friends,' he writes, 'keep your meetings, that in the Truth ye may reign, and in the Power spread it abroad. And keep in the Truth, that ye may see and feel the Lord's presence amongst you. Be for it valiant upon the earth, and know one another in the power of it.'[68] We must now ask what he believed to be happening in silent worship, why he felt this should be a group activity as well as a solitary one, and why he believed it was the prime Quaker witness to the power of God.

If Friends had not organized themselves into Meetings, there might well have been no persecution. Missionary gatherings were a common and much enjoyed feature of life in Cromwell's day; these might be rowdy, and not always encouraged by magistrates and clergy, but the welcome the wandering Quaker missionaries often received even from people 'well-placed' in society (as well as the almost ritual disruption by undergraduates in Oxford and Cambridge) showed that they had a familiar role. It was the continuing meetings of those convinced of Fox's message which aroused alarm. The Meeting at Reading, for instance, was repeatedly raided by the local magistrate till all its adult members had been thrown into the local gaol; yet the children continued to gather at the place of meeting. Why did their parents not sit silent, each at home, and so avoid notice?

A sociologist might suggest that Fox was founding an

institution, a group of people who evolve procedures designed to secure the solidarity and preservation of their common identity. At times this has been true of the Society of Friends. But in its earliest years, the picture is different. At the beginning, Fox travelled from place to place, proclaiming his discovery; and in his wake people began to meet for worship. Sometimes it was years before he came back. Sometimes the practice of silent worship had begun before he arrived. In one of the most striking stories, a handful of Scottish soldiers who spent a short period on a warship worshipped in this way. This was in 1654, when there was no formal Quaker body in Scotland; the first travelling Friends came there in that year. Some months after they left the ship, two of the sailors began to meet in silent worship. They were savagely harrassed by the petty officers and captain (who was a nonconformist preacher) and mocked by the other men. Yet their numbers grew; and their mutual love and their efficiency in their duties won the respect of their persecutors. It was one of these who joined them, Thomas Lurting, who discovered in the middle of a battle that he could no longer take life—an independent discovery of the Quaker 'peace testimony' when he had never met a true Quaker. The practice of worship in this way was something more than a sociologist's 'ritual'.

Fox writes: 'This is to all who would learn silent waiting upon God and silent meeting. None that is upon the earth shall ever come to God but as they come to that of God in them—the Light that God has enlightened them with. That is it which must guide every one's mind up to God . . . The Spirit leads to wait upon God in silence, and to receive from God.' To reach this principle dwelling in oneself is to come to peace out of all the confusion and 'bustlings' of this world, including the confusion of human rationalizing. 'Such shall find [more] mercy of God (when their minds are guided up to God, and their spirits and minds are quieted) in silent waiting upon God, in one half hour, more peace and satisfaction, than they have had from all other teachers of the world in all their life-time.'[69]

It is interesting that he does not feel a need to give practical advice as to what one should be doing in a silent meeting. So there is not a way to compare his 'method' with that of modern meditation techniques. Since Friends do not draw a sharp line between the secular and the sacred, few of them would baulk at the suggestion that the sense of relaxation gained by such techniques is a constituent of the peace Fox speaks of. Yet those Friends who practice yoga or transcendental meditation are clear that there is a difference; and though such practice is a helpful preparation for Quaker worship, it is not what one should be doing throughout the meeting. On one specific point—what to do about intrusive thoughts—Fox gives the same counsel which would be given today: don't struggle with them. 'After thou seest thy thoughts and the temptations, do not think but submit; and then Power comes . . . Stand still in the Light and submit to it, and the other will be hushed and gone; and then content comes. When temptations and troubles appear, sink down in that which is pure; and all will be hushed and fly away.'[70]

Apart from similar passages, Fox's writing on silent worship is like the writing of a composer or a psycho-analyst. We read the description, but look in vain to see how the magic is performed. The working of the trick eludes us in the simplicity of the description and we remain mystified. Finally we must come to see that this seeking is not like hide-and-seek, guessing where to look and knowing whom we shall find behind the curtain. 'Knowing the trick of it' is a function of the ego (to recall the terminology of a previous section); and it is the wisdom, the self-importance, the busy-ness, the anxieties of the ego which bar our progress. 'Wait upon God . . . see little, and know little, and have little, and see your emptiness, and see your nakedness, and barrenness, and unfruitfulness . . .'[71] Paul Tillich writes:

> Let us not forget that waiting is a tremendous tension. It precludes all complacency about having nothing,

> indifference or cynical contempt toward those who have something, and indulgence in doubt and despair. Let us not make our pride in possessing nothing a new possession. That is one of the great temptations of our time, for there are few things left which we can claim as possessions. And we surrender to the same temptation when we boast, in our attempt to possess God, that we do not possess him. The divine answer to such an attempt is utter emptiness. Waiting is not despair. It is the acceptance of our not having, in the power of that which we already have.[72]

Fox is not intentionally withholding information about worship which would help us. He urges us to a surrender of self, and an expectancy which is not greedy or demanding. He encourages us to move from our sense of unworthiness and emptiness to the apprehension of that Worth and Fulness by which we measure our own deficiency. He leads us to hope that this apprehension will have the quality of a personal encounter in which we feel ourselves judged but not condemned—our selfish selves are to die, but in that death we will find a fulness of life which we had never imagined was possible for us. We will gain a sense of peace, and that peace will accompany us through the most turbulent of life's experiences. And this, says Fox, is not an arm's length away from us all the time. If we lose hold of it, as Naylor found, it waits to renew itself within us; just as Jesus, crucified and buried, is said to have burst forth on the morning when his followers set out to visit his tomb.

When someone first attends a Quaker meeting, it may be with a profound sense of 'coming home', even though he or she does not have the theological framework which Fox uses to describe the experience. For another, it is more difficult; time drags, nothing is 'happening'. These are the people to whom Fox says: 'It is a strange life to you to come to be silent, you must come into a new world.' Their own wisdom, their own understanding 'must die in the silence'. For them the spoken word of others in the meeting may be needed, but 'the intent of all speaking is to bring people into the Life, and to walk in and possess the same, and to live in and enjoy it, and to feel God's presence. And that is in the silence (not in the wandering, whirling, tempestuous part of man or woman).'[73]

So one function of one's fellow worshippers is to mediate the Spirit when one's own pathway is temporarily blocked (and this does not only happen to newcomers). This may be by speaking, but it may be by unspoken love. Thus Robert Barclay writes:

> Such is the evident certainty of that divine strength that is communicated by thus meeting together, and waiting in silence upon God, that sometimes when one hath come in, who has been unwatchful and wandering in his mind, or suddenly out of the hurry of outward business, and so not inwardly gathered with the rest, so soon as he retires himself inwardly, this Power being in good measure raised in the whole meeting will suddenly lay hold upon his spirit, and wonderfully help to raise up the good in him and beget him into the sense of the same Power, to the melting and warming of his heart; even as the warmth would take hold upon a man that is cold coming to a stove, or as a flame will lay hold upon some little combustible matter being near unto it.[74]

Once again there is no need to invoke the supernatural to explain this, specially if telepathy (which is not uncommon in meetings for worship) is regarded as a natural phenomenon. But in seventeenth-century writing, with its sharper distinction between the things of God and the things of 'the world', we do at times find the claim that what happens in Quaker worship is extra-ordinary. Thus Fox writes: 'Earthly reason tells thee what thou shalt lose; hearken not to that . . .'[75] —while a modern Friend can say: 'God is above all the God of the normal. In the common facts and circumstances of life He draws near to us, quietly he teaches us in the routine of life's trifles, gently and unnoticed His guidance comes to us through the channels of "reason, judgement and determining circumstance".'[76]

Do we need to decide between them? Only, I think, in the way that Jung advises us to develop our neglected functions, to cultivate feeling and intuition if we rely too much on thinking and the senses (and vice versa), and to acknowledge that we can open ourselves to a greater wisdom than that of our conscious mind—and we can do this without arguing about its source. In the same way, Friends have found a power in the group experience which does not demand to be analysed.

Fox has another way of looking at the link between the individual experience and that of the group. The exercise of waiting is an exercise in obedience. Thomas Lurting draws on his experience in naval warfare to write: 'As *silence* is the first word of command in Martial Discipline, so it is in the Spiritual; for until that's come unto, the Will and Mind of God cannot be known, much less done.'[77] And the word which might come to a Friend in the stillness was (and is) often a word of command. Whose command, what obedience? In Fox's terms, it was obedience to Christ, who only in this way exercised his Kingship over the hearts of men. This explained the slight ambiguity in Jesus' phrase 'the Kingdom of Heaven': God's rule, and also God's community. 'The gospel, which is the Power of God, which you have received from the beginning,' Fox writes to 'Friends in England and all parts of the world', 'keep in it and the fellowship of it; in which there is neither sect nor schism, but an everlasting fellowship and an everlasting order.'[78] The worshipping group thus provides the physical expression of two related realities. Firstly the love that exists among God's people: 'By this the world shall know that you are my disciples, that you love one another,' says Jesus,[79] meaning (if we take him literally), that neither ritual nor priesthood, building nor creed, confirmation nor membership of the Society of Friends, identifies the Christian, but the quality of his personal relationships. Secondly the group expresses God's order, in this word's double sense of pattern and command. This is why Fox sees the Meeting as the fundamental Quaker witness to the nature and glory of God.

Lewis Benson has pointed out that this community is quite different from an ecclesiastical institution.[80] It comes into existence at the moment that a group of people enter together into a certain relationship with God—or, if this word still causes trouble, when a group agrees to meet and to wait and to seek in a certain way, and to trust what they find. It ceases when they finally disperse, or when they harden it into a tradition which loses direct contact with what they have found. But that Reality is not dependent on buildings, or dogmas, or tradition; it is always there, waiting for us, indeed (Fox would say) seeking for us. This is why the early Friends were so determined that the Church of Christ was not a building nor a social institution. It is something fragile and elusive, yet persistent and infinitely strong; men's greatest efforts to preserve it in their own strength have added nothing to its own powers of enduring. It is beautifully characterized in a famous passage by William Penn:

> The humble, meek, merciful, just, pious, and devout souls are everywhere of one religion; and when death has taken off the mask they will know one another, though the divers liveries they wear here makes them strangers. This world is a form; our bodies are forms; and no visible acts of devotion can be without forms. But yet the less form in religion the better, since God is a Spirit; for the more mental our worship, the more adequate to the nature of God; the more silent, the more suitable to the language of a Spirit.[81]

George Fox's structure for the Society of Friends was an attempt not to dim the Light of this Spirit; so he made the question of authority a matter for those who worshipped together. Even so it smacked too much of human organization for one fair-sized group, which broke away. That group has disappeared. But Fox's arrangements, though they preserved the Society, did not save it from becoming an institution. In America it went through the processes of controversy and splitting which have characterized the church at large. In Great Britain, it became, by the mid-nineteenth century, almost a parody of a sociologically defined institution, with a private language, peculiar dress, particular culture, and disownment of any who married outside the group. However it would be generally agreed that at the point where the Society was most concerned with its own identity, it no longer reflected the discoveries of its founders and the reasons for its existence. At that point, it might have died an actual death without our regretting it. For the Spirit still blows where it wills, in and outside the churches. The Kingdom of God cannot be destroyed by the demise of any institution that bears its name. However, in the case of the Quakers, there has been a painful struggle to recapture something of the original vision, without elevating its founders into patriarchs. Its members today often express regret that they do not have the fire and certainty of Fox and Naylor, Penn and Barclay. But perhaps they have gained a certain humility, an acknowledgment of doubt and inadequacy, which serves the ideal in its own way.

* * *

The Voice of Christ

It is the work of a prophet to open spiritual truths to people; and show them things to come; to show them the joy and the judgement; the comfort and the sorrow; the ways of the Lord and the ways of the wicked; and that which they should walk in and that which they should not.

So Christ is a prophet—this great prophet that is raised up by the Lord; who in the midst of his church opens to his people—by his Power and by his Spirit and by his Light—opens to them things to come, and shows them the way of salvation, and shows them the ways of destruction, and the ways of life and the way of death.

So, where two or three are gathered in his name, there he is in the midst of them, exercising his prophetic office by his Power and by his Spirit. People who believe in the Light, as Christ has commanded, hear him, their prophet, speaking unto them, showing them the glory that is of the Father and himself.

A collected set of passages from George Fox's writings,
edited to be read aloud by Hugh McGregor Ross
(Unpublished, available Friends House Library, London)

Keep to that of God in you, which will lead you up to God when you are still from your own thoughts and imaginations, and desires and counsels of your own hearts, and motions, and wills; when you stand single from all these, waiting upon the Lord, your strength is renewed. He that waits upon the Lord feels his Shepherd, and he shall not want. And that which is of God within everyone is that which brings them together to wait upon God, which brings them to unity, which joins their hearts together up to God. So, as this moves, this is not to be quenched, when it moves to pray or speak; for there is the Power of the Lord.

Gospel Truth Demonstrated (1706) p. 101

Inward Peace

There is none upon the earth that come to have their spirits quieted but who come to the Light that Christ Jesus hath enlightened them withal; and so comes every spirit here to have a peculiar satisfaction and quietness in his own mind, and here comes the weary to have rest in Christ.

Gospel Truth Demonstrated (1706) p. 96

Wandering Thoughts

So after long travel, strong cries, and many bitter tears and groans, I found a little hope springing in me, that the Lord in his own time would bring forth his Seed . . . to rule in me; and this was given me at a time when a sense of my unworthiness had so overwhelmed me in sorrow and anguish, that I thought myself unworthy of any of the creatures; forasmuch as I was out of the Covenant of God . . . Then did the hope of the resurrection of the just spring in me, and I was taught to wait on God, and to eat and drink in fear and watchfulness, showing forth the Lord's death till he should come to be raised to live and reign in me . . . And upon a time, being weary of my own thoughts in the meeting of God's people, I thought none was like me, and it was but vain to sit there with such a wandering mind as mine was while, though I laboured to stay it, yet could not as I would. At length, I thought to go forth; and as I was going the Lord thundered through me, saying: 'That which is weary must die.' So I turned to my seat and waited in the belief of God for the death of that part which was weary of the work of God . . . And the cross of Christ was laid upon me, and I bore it. And as I came willingly to take it up, I found it to be that thing which I had fought from my childhood, even the power of God . . .

Stephen Crisp, *Journal* (1655) p. 18

True Prayer

And concerning praying in the Spirit; which Spirit makes intercession to God, with sighs and groans which cannot be uttered. Now where this Spirit is prayed in (which all true prayer is to be in) it makes intercession through the veils, through the clouds and thick darkness, by the invisible Power, to the invisible God.

Epistle 312 (1674)

That which calls your minds out of the earth turns it towards God, where the pure Babe is born in the virgin-mind . . .

Epistle 56 (1653)

The priesthood of all men and women

What, are all true Christians priests?

Yes.

What, are women priests?

Yes, women priests.

And can men and women offer sacrifices without they wear the holy garments?

No.

What are the holy garments men and women must wear?

The fine linen; and they must go in white.

What, is this the priest's surplice?

Nay . . . it is the Righteousness of Christ, which is the righteousness of the saints; this is the royal garment of the royal priesthood, which everyone must put on, men and women. *Epistle 249* (1667)

Dr Craddock said 'You marry, but I know not how.'

Then I said unto him, 'It may be so', but why did he not come and see. Then he threatened how he had and would use his power against us. But I bid him take heed for he was an old man. Then I asked him where did ever any priest from Genesis to Revelation marry any. If he could show me any instance we would come to [the priests] to marry us.*

'For thou hast excommunicated one of my friends two years after he was dead, about it. And why dost not excommunicate Issac and Jacob, and Boaz and Ruth, and Christ and his disciples for going to a marriage? Why dost thou not use thy power against them; for we do not read that they were ever married by the priests; but they took one another in the assemblies of the righteous, in the presence of God and his people; and so do we. And we have all the holy men and women of our side, that the Scripture speaks of in this practice.'

Journal (1667) p. 500

* Friends believed that only God, and no human agency, could solemnize a marriage. From 1653, or even earlier, they took one another as husband and wife in front of the witnessing meeting, without recourse to priest or magistrate.

The Mountain and the Temple

And in the afternoon there was a great gathering of people . . . and so the [chapel] would not hold them, and so I was moved to go upon a mountain hard by, and the people gathered to the mountain and sat down; though it was then a strange thing to have meetings elsewhere than in the church (so-called) because it was holy ground, they thought. People were so ignorant then. So after some time I stood up, and said unto them that the ground was as holy as any other, and that Christ did meet upon a mountain, and by the seaside, and in houses, and so did his apostles and disciples; and though the Jews had a temple called holy in the old testament and a worship there, yet Christ had ended that temple and worship and set up a worship in Spirit and Truth, and all the true believers in Christ that received him and his gospel of life and salvation were the true Christians, and their bodies were the temples of God and Christ and the Holy Ghost.

Preface to *The Memory of the Righteous Revived* (1689)

'Mumming and Dumbing'

And many received the Lord's truth in their hearts and came to sit under Christ's teaching. And the priests and professors would come to our meetings, and Friends would be sitting silent in his Power and Truth and feeling him among them, and they would say, 'Look how the people sit mumming and dumbing here; here is no edification'; and then it hath been said [by us], 'Let the priest look to his own parish, how the people sit mumming and dumbing all their lifetime under him, always under his teaching that they may be always paying him; and why should we not sit under Christ, our Prophet, Shepherd, Bishop and Priest and hear him? We are not to speak our own words, but if he gives us any thing, we are to speak it faithfully'.

A History of the Rise of Friends and Progress of Truth (1690)

The Good Within

The Apostle saith to the believers, 'Try all things, hold fast to that which is good'. So you, holding fast that which is good, with that you can try all things, whether they be good or bad. 'And be not overcome with evil, but overcome evil with good'; this is the command. So it is the good that must overcome the evil; and what hath the children of God to overcome the evil withal, but the good? Therefore then, all must hold fast that which is good . . . but when any do go from the good in themselves, they are not like[ly] with it to overcome the evil, nor with it try all things.

Epistle 398 (1684)

True and False Liberty

Dear Friends and brethren in Jesus Christ, in whom ye all have Peace and Life, in whom there is no division, schism, rent, strife nor separation; for Christ is not divided, and there can be no separation in the Truth, nor in the Light, Grace, Faith and Holy Ghost, but unity, fellowship and communion. For the devil was the first that went out of the Truth, separated from it, and tempted man to disobey God, and to go from the Truth into a false liberty, to do that which God forbad. So it is the serpent now that leads men and women into a false liberty, even the god of the world, from which man and woman must be separated by the Truth, that Christ the Truth may make them free and then they are free indeed. Then they are to stand fast in that liberty in which Christ hath made them free, and in him there is no division, schism, rent nor separation; but Peace, Life, and reconciliation to God and to one another. So in Christ male and female are one: for whether they be male or female, Jew or Gentile, bond or free, they are all one in Christ . . .

Keep in the word of wisdom which is gentle, pure and peaceable, and in the word of patience that endureth and beareth all things; which word of patience the devil and the world and all his instruments can never wear out; it will wear them all out, for it was before they were and will be when they are gone, the pure holy word of God, by which all God's children are born again, and feed on the milk thereof, and live and grow by it. My desires are that ye may all be of one heart, mind, soul and spirit in Christ Jesus, Amen. G.F.

Letter (1686) in *Journal* (Ellwood's edition, p. 602)

GEORGE FOX, THE MAN

I do not propose to tell the rest of the story of George Fox's life here, with his extensive travels in America, Ireland, Holland and Germany. His own vivid accounts of a few incidents are given in this book, and the reader who wants to learn more should turn to his Journal. But there are aspects of him not yet described, which we learn partly from other sources; one of these, William Penn's appreciation, is quoted later. This was written at the time of his death; and perhaps love and the passage of time have softened the impression of asperity which Fox sometimes gives in his younger days, for instance in this letter to a persecuting magistrate: 'O Lawson, O blood sucker, O Esau . . . O thou serpent who are painted outwardly with the saint's words, but a murderer and killer of the just, O thou viper . . . Neither count this hard language, nor revile at it, it's the love of the Lord God to thee.'[82]

Fox could be angry as well as stern; but in the main it was a generous anger. After rounding on a groom for stealing his horse's oats he adds: 'I had rather they had robbed me.'[83] Most of the dispraise we have of him occurs in bitter controversial writing, often in a tone which makes his letter to Sir Thomas Lawson look almost mild. The imputations are often so wild as to disprove themselves: for instance that he charmed people to follow him by tying ribbons on them. Their rancour is more than balanced by testimonies to the love in which he was held, not least by some who had begun as his enemies, such as the governor of Scarborough Castle where he was ill-treated in prison. Next time he came to Scarborough, 'the governor heard I was come to town and sent to me by one of his soldiers, and said surely I would not be so unkind as not to come and see him and his wife. So after meeting was done I went up to visit him, and he was very courteous and loving.'[84] An unusual experience for a discharged convict!

At times the love and respect shown to him seem as excessive in their phraseology as that shown to James Naylor. But Fox's scruples can be seen in the crossing-out and correction of the more extreme phrases in letters to him, while at the same time we can admire his honesty in preserving these papers intentionally for the use of future historians, though they are not all to his credit. Though uneducated himself, he laid the foundations for a truthful and extensive Quaker history.

The magnetism which he had over others was not used to manipulate or control them. Penn says, 'He exercised no authority but over evil . . .' but that was so compelling that more than once people cried 'Take thy eyes off me!' The appeal of his style of speaking may be judged from many of the extracts in this book, if they are read aloud, fairly slowly; for most of them were dictated extempore, and bear little sign of being polished by him afterwards. (His editors worked them over after his death, but original manuscripts or printings are often available for comparison.) His style moves easily from the vivid and homely to the grander tones of the Authorized Version; he often relies on repetition for emphasis, even to the point of creating a rough poetry. His words still come to life and touch the heart, where the sermons of many famous preachers (for instance John Wesley) lie dead on the page. We have records of his spoken ministry in meetings for worship. This is occasionally very brief, but more often of a length which would seem unfamiliar in most Quaker meetings today. It is usually a powerful concentration on a single theme, or two themes cogently contrasted. But at times it ranges in a kind of free association over several apparently unrelated topics.

I have already referred to his dry sense of humour. He must have been devastating in court when he was pointing out the flaws in a badly-drawn indictment, or questioning a confused opponent. His Journal abounds in little touches which bring the personalities in a scene to life. But he disapproved of excessive hilarity, seeing it as a defence against the serious demands of our existence. This has given him a rather grim image, which I think he does not deserve, since there are many indications that people sought out his company and enjoyed it.

His reputation has also suffered from those passages in his Journal where he seems to take a delight in recording when sickness or disgrace, 'the judgement of the Lord', overtakes someone who had opposed him. However we should set against this the occasions when he had it in his power to bring an assailant to court, and was even encouraged to do so by the representatives of the law; but it was his principle not to do so. Though he would not budge an inch to compromise with an opponent, his aim was always to reach his heart. When this happens, Fox does not take personal credit for it, but gives the glory to God. In the same way, he feels it is his duty to record the fate of those who turned their backs on Truth, but not to dwell on this. 'Several strange and sudden judgements came upon many of these conspirators against me which would be too large to declare.'[85] Whatever the modern reader may surmise about his unconscious satisfaction, Fox is careful to say that one should leave one's personal feelings behind when one is wronged: 'All such spirits I laid before the Lord, and left them to him to deal with.' The record of his actions amply confirms this. He comments on the paradox of the sinfulness of human revenge and the justice of God, when he is recording the bloodbath among the judges which followed the restoration of Charles II. 'This was sad work, destroying of people, contrary to the nature of Christians who have the nature of lambs and sheep. But there was a secret hand in bringing this day upon that hypocritical generation of professors, who, being got into power, grew proud, haughty, and cruel beyond others, and persecuted the people of God without pity.'[86]

His own sense of pity was profound: for children, prisoners, servants and slaves; for the sick and the persecuted; for ordinary people, starved in their spiritual lives. He 'could speak a word in due season to the conditions and capacities of most, especially to them that were weary and wanted soul's rest', according to the testimony of his step-daughters.[87] Fox recalls arriving at a house, 'and there was a boy lying in the cradle which they rocked, about eleven years old. He was grown almost double, and I cast my eye upon the boy and seeing he was dirty, I bid the lass wash his face and his hands and get him up and bring him to me. So she brought him to me and I bid her take him and wash him again, for she had not washed him clean, then I was moved of the Lord God to lay my hands upon him and speak to him . . .'[88]

Fox was a practical man of wide-ranging interests. His letters include advice to Friends on business affairs, making wills, treatment of servants and natives in the colonial plantations, the rehabilitation of beggars and the care of those in need. In common with many great democrats in theory and practice, he liked to manage and advise. And yet he was aware of this discrepancy, and of the need to bring people to 'follow their own Teacher'. A letter to his son-in-law about the conversion of a property into a Friends' meeting house illustrates these warring traits, and also his delight in practical details:

> And as concerning the meeting place itself, whether the barn or the house, I shall leave to you. But if the barn will do better, if you could make it wider, maybe it may be better, because then there will be the house to go into . . . And the yards are low which may be raised and laid dry, and you have stones enough, and poor men to get them . . . And I would have all the thatch pulled off all the houses and laid in a heap to rot for manure to be laid upon the close . . . But these things I must leave to you.[89]

I have mentioned the letters to the King, to the Pope, to the Kings of Austria, France and Spain, the Great Turk, the Emperor of China, and even the legendary Prester John, all offering spiritual counsel with sublime confidence. 'Speaking Truth to power' was seen as an important aspect of Quaker witness ever since Fox (then a prisoner) had first lectured Cromwell on the need for rulers to be open to God's Truth:

> And as I was turning, he catched me by the hand and said these words with tears in his eyes, 'Come again to my house; for if thou and I were but an hour in a day together we should be nearer one to the other', and that he wished me no more ill than he did to his own soul. And I told him if he did he wronged his soul . . . Then I was brought into a great hall, where the Protector's gentlemen were to dine . . . I bid them let the Protector know I would not eat a bit of his bread, nor sup of his drink. When he heard this, he said there was a people risen, meaning us, that he could not win either with honours, high places or gifts, but all other people he could.[90]

Fox was then thirty-one, Cromwell fifty-six.

George Fox was very concerned for education, set up one school himself, and advised the foundation of several more, some of which were for girls (an unconventional view at that time). He bequeathed some land which William Penn had given him in Pennsylvania to the city of Philadelphia, '. . . to build a meeting house for the use of Friends, and a schoolhouse upon another part, and to enclose another part for a garden, and to plant it with all sorts of physical plants for lads and lasses to learn simples there, and the uses to convert them to—distilled waters, oils, ointments, &c.'[91] He was part author of a schoolbook called *Instructions for Right Spelling and Plain Directions for Reading and Writing English, with Several Delightful Things very Useful and Necessary for Young and Old to Learn*—though his own manuscripts make it obvious that he didn't compile the section 'Words Alike in Sound but Spelled Differently'! He showed a harmless vanity in the knowledge he had managed to acquire.

This and his advocacy of 'plain language', that is the use of the familiar 'thou' to everyone without distinction of social standing, led to an interest in grammar and linguistics. One result of this was another book, *The Battledoor,* in which he had a small part, showing the usage of 'thou' in some thirty-five languages. His first letter to the Ottoman Sultan, the 'Grand Turk', is a conventional harangue, which, if it had ever arrived, could hardly have made an impression. But later ones quote extensively from the Koran, to show the universal nature of the Light. He also advocated translation of the Bible, and Quaker treatises, into every language. 'Are not the scriptures of the new testament and new covenant to be translated, and to be read, spoken and interpreted in every man's language and mother-tongue? . . This world's god' (that is, the devil) 'and his followers would keep people ignorant from the scriptures.'[92]—He once astonished a courtroom by thundering out 'Thou shalt not swear' in Hebrew.

He was deeply read in the Bible. A contemporary said that if every Bible in England were destroyed the book could have been reconstructed from his memory. His use of it in controversy shows an understanding of the spirit of its teaching unlike the arid text-slinging of much religious dispute at the time. We may recall that Jesus too was deeply read in Jewish scripture, and saw it as the record of a spiritual development, when many of his contemporaries saw it only as nationalist history and a body of conventional observances.

Fox's scrupulous tact and honesty are seen in the circumstances of his marriage in 1669 to Margaret Fell, whose home at Swarthmore Hall in Lancashire had been a centre for the Quaker movement since Fox and Naylor had visited it together in 1652. He first enquired of the children of her first marriage to ensure that they would not suffer financial loss if she remarried; and he executed a deed renouncing his legal right as her husband to her property. This marriage, to a wealthy judge's widow, much older than him and of a very different social background, was another cause of scandal to those who wished to disapprove. Fox was very careful to wait until Friends were clear in their minds that he and Margaret were acting rightly.

Though they were seldom together, their letters show this marriage to have been a deep and loving one. To give one touching instance, when he was imprisoned at Worcester, she sent him some money to buy himself some comforts, and he spent 'a pretty deal' of it to buy and send her material for a new dress instead.

He is reticent about his own sources of money, and not much is known. It seems that even as a young man he had enough for his needs with some to give away to the unfortunate. In later life we hear of him investing in ships. He was a man of very modest tastes, but he did not preach or practice an exaggerated puritanism. This is shown in a letter to his wife from one of her daughters, which also indicates the family's affection for George. (Incidentally, Sarah Fell seems to be having some trouble in remembering to say 'thou' for 'you'!)

> We desire to know as soon as thou can when we may expect you with our dear father for several reasons as thou may well know; and thou should buy us a cask of wine, of what sort thou judges father like best, for we have none, only some cider and March beer bottled up; also you should buy us some anchovies, some olives and two larding needles, and some oranges and lemons, and what else you think fit. And pray let us know some certainty of your coming as soon as you can.[93]

In the days of the Commonwealth, Friends were not conspicuous for asceticism, though they tried (and most of them were obliged) to live simply. Within the much more permissive Restoration culture, they were led to a strong witness for moderation and simplicity in dress, eating, drinking, and every use of the gifts of the creation. Since every word one spoke should be as sacred as an oath, every meal a sacrament, every day a holy-day, it was natural that they should condemn the licentious painting, music and theatre of the 1660s, the elaborate and artificial manners of the gentry, the love of rich dishes, jewels and expensive clothes, the luxuries of 'madmen who destroy the creation'. But this was not, at first, a set of rules. How could it be, among a group whose message was 'gospel liberty and the royal law of love' (to quote the title of one of Fox's tracts)? But gradually, after Fox's death in 1691, Quakers began to conform to the image which was to become a tradition, the uniform grey clothes, the quaint formal language (descended from that 'plain speech' which had seemed over-familiar to its first hearers!) and an aversion to art, music and sociable living. This would have been castigated by George Fox as 'running out into forms'; and it was vigorously denounced by Margaret Fox at the end of her long life:

> We are now running into that which Christ cried Woe against, minding altogether outward things . . . We must look at no colours, nor make anything that is changeable colours as the hills are, nor wear them; but we must be all in one dress and one colour; this is a silly poor gospel . . .[94]

Some Friends today feel that in this way, as well as in the growing mistrust of 'enthusiasm', their Society lost its grip on some of its basic insights during the eighteenth and nineteenth centuries; just as General Booth of the Salvation Army is said to have asked why God could not keep a movement pure for more than one generation. A fuller insight into the lives of Quakers in those later times might stop one making this judgement too glibly. But in the twentieth century, we can see a general move in Christianity towards many of the affirmations of George Fox and his friends: in charismatic experience, in the growing mistrust of dogma, and in a new interpretation of the relationship of God, the individual and society. This is too large a statement to justify here, but it may be of interest to conclude with a few modern quotations from diverse origins, to compare with what Fox believed and expressed.

Bede Griffiths is a Roman Catholic monk living in a Christian community in India which follows the customs of a Hindu ashram and adapts itself to Hindu and Buddhist ways of thought. He writes:

> In that stillness, in that silence, the Word is hidden, the Word in which every thing exists eternally in the plenitude of being. And in that Word the Spirit is present, the Spirit which is in all creation and in the heart of every man, and in our own inmost being. And that Spirit is Love, a love which penetrates every atom in the universe, which fills every living thing, which moves in the heart of every man, which gathers all into unity. In that Spirit we are all one in the Word, each one unique in himself, reflecting the Light of the Word, and in that Word we are one with the Father, the Source of all. 'That they may all be one; even as thou, Father, art in me, and I in thee, that they also may be in us'.[95]

Harry Williams, the Anglican monk and writer, says:

> I shall find God within me all right. I shall find the love and joy and peace which is my truest self. But the discovery will for a long time be mixed up with the discomforts of the journey. What in due time will happen is that slowly (though not gradually but by fits and starts) I shall become more aware of God's presence within and less aware of the turmoil of the journey because, having found my truest self as God's presence within me, I shall be able to accept and receive the more superficial aspects of myself with less difficulty and pain. And the more I am thus able to accept and receive the more superficial aspects of myself, the less important will they be and the less harm will they do. They will begin to diminish and even disappear. In the end . . . I shall be so aware of God's presence within me that the rest of me will be totally transfigured by it.[96]

Hans Küng, the radical Roman Catholic theologian, writes of Jesus' relation to the society of his day in words that could be applied almost unaltered to the early Friends, and relates to the dilemma of choice for Christians today:

> There was his oddly radical identification of God's cause with man's; to what tremendous consequences in theory and practice this had led. He had been aggressive on all sides, now he was attacked on all sides. He had not played any of the expected roles: for those who supported law and order he turned out to be a provocateur, dangerous to the system. He disappointed the activist revolutionaries by his non-violent love of peace. On the other hand he offended the passive world-forsaking ascetics by his uninhibited worldliness. And for the devout who adapted themselves to the world he was too uncompromising. For the silent majority he was too noisy and for the noisy minority he was too quiet, too gentle for the strict and too strict for the gentle. He was an obvious outsider in a critically dangerous social conflict: in opposition both to the prevailing conditions and those who opposed them.[97]

John A. T. Robinson, later Bishop of Woolwich, writes:

> The Holy Communion is the great workshop of the new world where the 'we who are many' are recreated as the true, the new community in Christ. And the holy community known at the liturgy is only, as it were in inset, the norm of what has to be made true of all society. Here indeed is the 'classless society' in which there is neither Jew nor Greek, male nor female, bond nor free. We are not called to 'bring in' the Kingdom of God, but to bring it out from where we have known it. Our task is not to 'build' what does not yet exist, but to 'build up' what is already there, that cell of the new society which is present, or should be present, whenever two or three are gathered together in Christ's name.[98]

Paul Tillich discusses the words and context of the saying in John's gospel, 'He that doeth the Truth cometh to the Light'.

> 'Doing the Truth', 'being of the Truth', 'the Truth has come', 'I am the Truth'—all these combinations of words indicate that Truth in Christianity is something that *happens,* something that is bound to a special place, to a special time, to a special personality. Truth is something new, something which is *done* by God in history, and, because of this, something which is *done* in the individual life . . . In Greek thought, truth can only be found. In Christianity Truth is found if it is done and done if it is found . . . The decision for or against Truth is *the* life-or-death decision, and this decision is identical with the decision in which Christ is accepted or rejected. You cannot have *opinion* about the Christ after you have faced him. You can only do the Truth by following him, or do the lie by rejecting him.[99]

In contrast to the external authority, whether of priest or bible, preached by all the churches of his day, Fox taught another authority, known within, and a way to find and follow it. 'Wait in the Light to receive the Power' thus lies at the heart of his message—not the secret of a few mystics, but a starting point for all men. We may compare Metropolitan Anthony Bloom, writing on prayer for 'those who cannot pray':

> There is a story of an old peasant who used to spend hours and hours sitting in the chapel motionless, doing nothing. The priest said to him 'What are you doing all these hours?' The old peasant said 'I look at Him, He looks at me and we are happy.' This can be reached only if we learn a certain amount of silence. Begin with the silence of the lips, with the silence of the emotions, the silence of the mind, the silence of the body. But it would be a mistake to imagine that we can start at the highest end, with the silence of the heart and the

> mind. We must start by silencing our body in the sense of learning to keep still, to let tenseness go, not to fall into daydreaming and slackness, but to use the formula of one of our Russian saints, to be like a violin string, wound in such a way that it can give the right notes, neither wound too much to breaking point, nor too little so that it only buzzes. And from then onward we must learn to listen to silence, to be absolutely quiet, and we may, more often than we imagine, discover that the words of the *Book of Revelation* come true: 'I stand at the door and knock'.[100]

But George Fox was not a 'modern' born out of his due time. He was very much a seventeenth-century man, in some ways a rather naive one: 'It was a noted thing generally amongst people that when I came, still I brought rain, and it had been so for many years'.[101] He does not give answers to all the questions that torment us; some of them he would not understand at all. Nor did he set himself up to give answers, though he was sure where answers could be found. His deeper insights are capable of development and rediscovery, perhaps infinitely, for they touch the centre of all men's religious experience. To every quotation, modern, Quaker or biblical, his rejoinder would be the personal challenge: 'Christ saith this, and the apostles say this; but what canst thou say?'

* * *

William Penn remembers George Fox

He was a man that God endued with a clear and wonderful depth, a discerner of others' spirits, and very much a master of his own. And though the side of his understanding that lay next the world, and especially the expression of it, might sound uncouth and unfashionable to nice ears, his matter was nevertheless very profound; and would not only bear to be often considered but the more it was so the more weighty and instructing it appeared. And abruptly and brokenly as sometimes his sentences would fall from him about divine things, it is well known they were often as texts to many fairer declarations. And indeed it showed, beyond all contradiction, that God sent him, that no arts or parts had any share in his matter or manner of his ministry; and that so many great, excellent and necessary truths as he came forth to preach to mankind had nothing of man's wit or wisdom to recommend them; so that as to man he was an original, being no man's copy. And his ministry and writings show they are from one that was not taught of man, nor had learned what he said by study. Nor were they notional or speculative, but sensible and practical truths, tending to conversion and regeneration and the setting up of the Kingdom of God in the hearts of men; and the way of it was his work.

From the clearness of the principle, the power and efficiency of it, in the exemplary sobriety, plainness, zeal, steadiness, humility, gravity, punctuality, charity, and circumspect care in the government of church affairs, which shined in his and their life and testimony that God employed in this work, it greatly confirmed me that it was of God, and engaged my soul in a deep love, fear, reverence, and thankfulness for his love and mercy therein to mankind; in which mind I remain and shall, I hope, to the end of my days.

In his testimony or ministry, he much laboured to open Truth to the people's understandings, and to bottom them upon the principle and principal, Christ Jesus, the Light of the world, that by bringing them to something of God in themselves, they might the better know and judge of him and themselves.

He had an extraordinary gift in opening the scriptures. He would go to the marrow of things, and show the mind, harmony, and fulfilling of them with much plainness, and to great comfort and edification . . .

But above all he excelled in prayer. The inwardness and weight of his spirit, the reverence and solemnity of his address and behaviour, and the fewness and fulness of his words, have often struck even strangers with admiration, as they used to reach other with consolation. The most awful, living, reverent frame I ever felt or beheld, I must say, was his in prayer. And truly it was a testimony that he knew and lived nearer to the Lord than other men; for they that know him most will see most reason to approach him with reverence and fear . . .

He exercised no authority but over evil, and that everywhere and in all, but with love, compassion and long-suffering, as ready to forgive as unapt to take offence . . . For in all things he acquitted himself like a man, yea, a strong man, a new and heavenly-minded man, a divine and a naturalist, and all of God Almighty's making.

William Penn in the Preface to Ellwood's edition of George Fox's *Journal* (1694)

An Opponent Converted

And there came on Colonel Rous, a justice of peace, with a great company [to visit us in the prison]. And he was as full of words and talk as ever I heard a man in my life, so as there was no speaking to him; so at last I asked him, to stop him, whether he had ever been at school and knew what belonged to questions and answers.

'At school!' said he, 'yes.'

'At school!' said the soldiers. 'Doth he say so to our Colonel that is a scholar?'

'Then,' said I, 'if he be so, let him be still and receive answers from me to what he hath said.'

And so he was desired to hold his peace, or see if he could hold his peace a little while, till Truth were spoken to him. And then the Light was spoken of to him (which let him see his sinful life that he had lived in, and his words and his ways), that would be his Teacher to lead him from them, if he minded it, and his condemnation if he acted against it. And if he had anything to speak he might speak.

And he was stricken dumb and his mouth was shut, and he cast his head up and down and his face swelled, and he could not speak for a good space. His face was as red as a turkey. And his lips rent and he mumbled, and the people thought he would have fallen down. And I stepped to him; and he said, 'I was never so in my life before.' For the Lord's power stopped the evil power and air in him and almost choked him.

And for ever after the man was very loving to Friends . . .

Journal (1656) p. 251

Elections in London

A little before the time for choosing new sheriffs for the city, those who put up to be chosen desiring our Friends to give their voices for them, I wrote a few lines tending to discover what spirit they were of, and how they stood affected to true liberty; it was by way of enquiry, thus: Do any here in London, that stand to be chosen sheriffs, own that Christ who was crucified without the gates of Jerusalem, to be the Light of the world that 'enlightens every man that cometh into the world', who saith 'Believe in the Light that ye may become children of the Light'? Is any of you against persecuting people for their religion and worship of God (in Spirit, as Christ commanded)? For Christ said, 'I am not of this world, nor my Kingdom'; therefore he doth not uphold his spiritual worship and pure religion with worldly and carnal weapons. Christ said, 'Swear not at all'; and his apostle James saith the same: but will you not force us to break Christ's and his apostle's commands, in putting oaths to us? Christ saith to his apostles, 'Freely ye have received, freely give.' Will not you force us to give tithes and maintenance to such teachers as we know God hath not sent? Shall we be free to serve and worship God and keep his and his Son's commands, if we give our voices freely for you? For we are unwilling to give our voices for such as will imprison and persecute us, and spoil our goods . . .

. . . And to the people: . . . Live in that love of God [in which] ye will seek the good and peace of all men and the hurt of no man . . . *Journal* (1682) (Ellwood's edition p. 554)

Social Relationships
All Friends everywhere, take heed of wronging the world or anyone in bargains, or overreaching them, but dwell in the cool, sweet and holy power of the Lord God.

Epistle 131 (1656)

People in the world will say 'How do you do, sir?'; doff the hat, scrape a leg, make a curtsey; 'I am glad to see you well', 'Your servant, my lord (or sir) or mistress'; and when they are past them, with the same tongue wish evil to them, speak evil of them . . . and laugh at one another behind their backs . . .

These salutations are vain and not to be observed . . . that plainness and truth and uprightness and honesty may come to rule in people . . . that the witness of God in all may arise that leads to Truth in the inward parts.

Gospel Truth Demonstrated (1706) p. 107

The Right Attitude to the World's Resources
Away with you, say the professors and teachers of the world, you are a company of mad men, you are not fit to live upon the earth.

Aye but, say the serious people, you are the madmen that destroy the creation and the creatures of God, upon your lusts and the lusts of your eye, the lusts of the flesh, and the pride of life, which is not of the Father but of the world; by which you destroy the Father's works and the prime of the creatures, which were given forth to be used by the Wisdom by which they were created to the glory of the Creator . . . The Quakers are come into the Wisdom of God, by which all things were created; so that if they eat and drink, it must be to the praise and glory of God, being in his fear; so they cannot have fellowship with the destroyers and marrers of the workmanship of God, and the creation.

Gospel Truth Demonstrated (1706) pp. 158 and 160

George Fox's knowledge of Scripture

I declared unto them that Adam and Eve were perfect before they fell, and all that God made was perfect, and the imperfection came by the Devil and the fall. And Christ that came to destroy the Devil said, 'Be ye perfect'. But one of the professors said that Job said, 'What! Shall mortal man be more pure than his Maker? The heavens are not clear in his sight. God charged his angels with folly.' But I showed him his mistake, that it was not Job that said so, but those which contended against Job. For Job stood for perfection and his integrity; and they were called miserable comforters.

Journal (1653) p. 166

Now Moses and Aaron and the seventy elders did not say to those assemblies of the women: 'We can do our work ourselves, and you are fitter to be at home to wash the dishes'; or such-like expressions. But they did encourage them in the work and service of God, in those things which God had commanded them in the time of the Law.

For God had poured his Spirit upon the house of Israel, to give them an understanding to do those things which God had commanded them; by which Spirit their hearts were stirred up to do God's work, both males and females.

Epistle 320 (1676) Commenting on *Exodus,* 38

To his Wife, after being arrested

8th of 12th month 1673

Dear Heart,

Thou seemed to be much grieved when I was speaking of prisons, and when I was taken thou began to fall upon me with blaming of me; and I told thee that I was to bear it, and why could not thee be content with the will of God? And thou said some words and then was pretty quiet, And thou was loath to go to Parker, but it was well thou did, and it had been well thou had been more over it* to me; for when I was at John Rous's I [fore-] saw that I was taken prisoner; and when I was at Bray D'Oyly's as I sat at supper, I saw I was taken the night before I was.

The three pound thou sent up to me, in love, for it I did speak to a Friend to send thee as much Spanish black cloth as will make thee a gown and it did cost us a pretty deal of money.

And I saw I had a winepress to tread, and the Lord's Power is over all, blessed be his name for ever; and not only so but the winepress is to be trodden among Friends where the Life is not lived in.

I hear of a ship of Thomas Edmonson's is cast away, which I had a part in, but let it go; and Thomas can give you or thee an account of all things. G.F.

Quoted in *Journal,* p. 681

Give God the Glory

About this time a pain struck into my shoulder, which gradually fell down into my arm and hand, so that the use thereof I was wholly deprived of; and not only so but my pain greatly increased both day and night. And for three months I could neither put my clothes on nor off myself, and my arm and hand began to wither, so that I did seek to some physicians for cure, but no cure could I get by any of them; until at last, as I was asleep upon my bed in the night time, I saw in a vision that I was with dear George Fox; and I thought I said unto him: 'George, my faith is such that if thou seest thy way to lay thy hand upon my shoulder, my arm and hand shall be whole throughout.' Which remained with me after I awaked, two days and nights, that the thing was a true vision and that I must go to G.F. until at last, through much exercise of mind, as a near and great trial of my faith, I was made willing to go to him; he being then at Swarthmore, in Lancashire, where there was a meeting of Friends, being on the first day of the week.

* i.e. if you had been more accepting, it would have been easier for me.

And some time after the meeting, I called him aside into the Hall, and gave him a relation of my concern as aforesaid, showing him my arm and hand; and in a little time, we walking together silent, he turned about, and looked upon me, lifting his hand and laid it on my shoulder, and said: 'The Lord strengthen thee both within and without.' And so we parted; and I went to Thomas Lower's of Marsh-Grange that night; and when I was sat down to supper in his house, immediately, before I was aware, my hand was lifted up to do its office, which it could not for so long, as aforesaid; which struck me into a great admiration; and my heart was broken into true tenderness before the Lord; and the next day I went home, with my hand and arm restored to its former use and strength, without any pain.

And the next time that G.F. and I met, he readily said: 'John, thou mended, thou mended.' I answered, 'Yes, very well, in a little time.' 'Well', said he, 'Give God the glory.'

John Banks in his *Journal* (1677) p. 66

Cherish the children of others

Now all you that do murmur against people that have many children, and do complain and say that they do fill your towns, cities and countries with children; and many times you that do so complain have few or no children, and you are afraid that they should come to want and then you must be fain to relieve their necessities. And what then? What you do give to the poor you lend to the Lord, and He will repay it to you again if they cannot; and this wanting mind is for want of faith in God, who gives the increase of all, and is rich unto all that call upon him. And the Lord would have you to take notice that children are the heritage of the Lord. And so what you do give to the breeding and nursing and relieving of children, you do it to the heritage of the Lord, and the Lord hath many adopted sons . . .

And what if you that have no children should do so? It was but a cross to the grumbling and murmuring self which many times have no children and are discontent with the poor that have many . . . And that will be a happy day when they come to nurse Christ's chickens, doves, lambs, babes and little children.

Gospel Truth Demonstrated (1706) p. 875

Finally, Margaret Fox's account of George Fox's first visit to her home, Swarthmore Hall.

In the year 1652 it pleased the Lord to draw him towards us . . . My then husband, Thomas Fell, was not at home at that time, but gone the Welsh circuit, being one of the Judges of Assize, and our house being a place open to entertain ministers and religious people at, one of George Fox's friends brought him hither, where he stayed all night. And the next day, being a lecture or a fast-day, he went to Ulverston steeplehouse, but came not in till people were gathered; I and my children had been there a long time before. And when they were singing before the sermon, he came in; and when they had done singing, he stood up upon a seat or form and desired that he might have liberty to speak. And he that was in the pulpit said he might. And the first words that he spoke were as followeth: 'He is not a Jew that is one outward, neither is that circumcision which is outward; but he is a Jew that is one inward, and that is circumcision which is of the heart.' And so he went on and said, How that Christ was the Light of the world and lighteth every man that cometh into the world; and that by this Light they might be gathered to God, etc. And I stood up in my pew, and I wondered at his doctrine, for I had never heard such before. And then he went on, and opened the Scriptures, and said, 'The Scriptures were the prophets' words and Christ's and the Apostles' words, and what as they spoke they enjoyed and possessed and had it from the Lord.' And said, 'Then what had any to do with the Scriptures, but as they came to the Spirit that gave them forth? You will say, Christ saith this, and the apostles say this; but what canst thou say? Art thou a child of Light and hast walked in the Light, and what thou speakest, is it inwardly from God?'

This opened me so that it cut me to the heart; and then I saw clearly we were all wrong. So I sat me down in my pew again, and cried bitterly. And I cried in my spirit to the Lord, 'We are all thieves, we are all thieves, we have taken the Scriptures in words and know nothing of them in ourselves.' So that served me, that I cannot well tell what he spake afterwards; but he went on in declaring against the false prophets and priests and deceivers of the people.

And there was one John Sawrey, a Justice of Peace and a professor, that bid the churchwarden 'Take him away' and he laid his hands upon him several times, and took them off again and let him alone; and then after while [George Fox] gave over and came to our house again that night . . . And I was stricken into such a sadness I knew not what to do, my husband being from home. I saw it was the Truth, and I could not deny it; and I did as the apostle saith, I 'received the Truth in the love of it.' And it was opened to me so clear that I have never a tittle in my heart against it; but I desired the Lord that I might be kept in it, and then I desired no greater portion.

The Testimony of Margaret Fox concerning her late husband (1694)

REFERENCES

[1] Christopher Hill, *The World Turned Upside Down,* Penguin, 1975, p. 361.
[2] Aldous Huxley, *The Perennial Philosophy,* Chatto & Windus, 1969, p. 223.
[3] George Fox, *Journal* ed. by J. L. Nickalls. London Yearly Meeting, 1952, rptd. 1975, p. 11. Entry for 1647.
[4] George Fox, *The True Christians Distinguished* (1689) ed. by Hugh Ross (Unpublished, available Friends House Library, London).
[5] Dante, *Paradiso,* canto xxxiii.
[6] Fox, *Journal,* op. cit., p. 19. Entry for 1647.
[7] Paul Tillich, *The Shaking of the Foundations,* Penguin, 1954, p. 151.
[8] Fox, *Journal,* op. cit., p. 35. Entry for 1648.
[9] *Christian Faith and Practice in the experience of the Society of Friends* (London Yearly Meeting, 1960) §14.
[10] Fox, *Journal,* op. cit., p. 37. Entry for 1649.
[11] *Ibid.,* p. 229. Entry for 1655.
[12] Richard Hubberthorne, *Works,* 1663, p. 271.
[13] *John,* 16:13.
[14] George Fox, *Gospel Truth Demonstrated,* 1706, p. 25.
[15] *Jeremiah,* 31:33–4.
[16] Robert Barclay, *An Apology for the True Christian Divinity . . .* 1676, Prop. II, section 7.
[17] See *The Original Vision* by Edward Robinson, and *A Sense of Presence* by Timothy Beardsworth, both published by the Religious Experience Research Unit, Oxford.
[18] Francis Howgill, *Works,* 1676, p. 35.
[19] Fox, Epistle 16 (1642).
[20] Fox, *Journal,* op. cit., p. 283. Entry for 1656, a letter.
[21] *Ibid.,* p. 19. Entry for 1647.
[22] Fox, Epistle 92 (1655).
[23] Fox, *Journal,* op. cit., p. 346. Entry for 1658, a letter to Cromwell's daughter, Lady Claypole.
[24] Fox, *Gospel Truth Demonstrated,* p. 1056.
[25] *Ibid.,* p. 273.
[26] Sigmund Freud, *New Introductory Lectures in Psychoanalysis,* Penguin Freud Library, vol. 2, 1973, p. 112.
[27] T. S. Eliot quoted without reference in *Experiment in Depth* by P. W. Martin. Routledge, 2nd edn., 1976, p. 188.
[28] William James, *The Varieties of Religious Experience,* Fount, 1977, p. 484.
[29] Carl G. Jung, *Memories, Dreams, Reflections,* Fontana, 1967, pp. 361–2, but the whole section should be consulted.
[30] Paul Tillich, *The Boundaries of our Being,* Fontana, 1973, p. 127.
[31] *John,* 1:9.
[32] Edward Robinson, *The Time-Bound Ladder,* Religious Experience Research Unit, p. 45.
[33] *Ibid.,* p. 41.

[34] Jung, op. cit., p.368–9.
[35] *Matthew,* 7:21.
[36] George Fox and James Naylor, *Saul's Errand to Damascus,* 1654, p. 32.
[37] *Matthew,* 28:20.
[38] Fox, Epistle 45 (1653).
[39] Fox, *Journal,* op. cit., p. 58. Entry for 1650, a paper.
[40] Jung, op. cit., p. 367.
[41] Fox, *Journal,* op. cit., p. 59. Entry for 1650, a paper.
[42] *Ibid.,* p. 184. Entry for 1655.
[43] *Ibid.,* p. 81. Entry for 1651.
[44] *Ibid.,* p. 481. Entry for 1664.
[45] Fox, Epistle 26 (1653).
[46] Anthony Storr, *Jung,* Fontana, 1973, pp. 88–9.
[47] *John,* 14:6.
[48] Carolyn Lee, 'Love bade me welcome but my soul drew back' in *The Friend,* 8 September 1978, p. 1118.
[49] Fox, *Journal,* op. cit., p. 283. Entry for 1656, a letter.
[50] *Romans,* 8:14 and 16, cited by Fox in Epistle 402 (1685) and elsewhere.
[51] Tillich, *The Boundaries of Our Being,* op. cit., p. 93.
[52] John Wesley, *Works,* vol. xiv, p. 360.
[53] *Joel,* 2:28.
[54] George Hickes, *The Spirit of Enthusiasm Exorcised,* 1680.
[55] Hill, op. cit., pp. 203 ff. and p. 232.
[56] William Penn in the Preface to George Fox's *Journal* (1694) p. xlix.
[57] 'The Testimony of Francis Howgill concerning Edward Burrough' the Preface to *The Memorable Works of a Son of Thunder* by Edward Burrough, 1672. The 'man of God' was Fox.
[58] From a letter (September 1656) published in *Early Quaker Writings* ed. by Barbour and Roberts, Norfolk Press, 1973, rptd. 1977, p. 480.
[59] From James Naylor's *Statement to a committee of the House of Commons,* 1656.
[60] James Naylor, *Works* (1716) p. xli.
[61] Ralph Farmer, *Satan Inthron'd,* 1656.
[62] William Dewsbury in a letter to Margaret Fell, 1659.
[63] See *The Beginnings of Quakerism* by William C. Braithwaite, 2nd edn. revised by Henry Cadbury, Sessions, 1955, rptd. 1970, pp. 354 and 438. See A Note on Sources, p. 117.
[64] William Dewsbury, *Works,* 1689, p. 219.
[65] Fox, *Journal,* op. cit., p. 491. Entry for 1665.
[66] Letter dated May 1666 in *Letters of Early Friends* ed. by A. R. Barclay, London: Harvey & Darton, 1841, p. 318.
[67] Fox, Epistle 264 (1669).
[68] Fox, Epistle 89 (1655).
[69] Fox, *Gospel Truth Demonstrated,* pp. 101 and 103.
[70] Fox, Epistle 10 (1652).
[71] Fox, Epistle 16 (1652).
[72] Tillich, *The Shaking of the Foundations,* op. cit., p. 153.
[73] Fox, *Gospel Truth Demonstrated,* p. 103.
[74] Barclay, op. cit., Prop. xi, section 7.
[75] Fox, Epistle 10 (1652).
[76] William Littleboy, *The Appeal of Quakerism to the Non-mystic,* 1916, p. 10, QHS rpt. 1964.

[77] Thomas Lurting, *The Fighting Sailor Turned Peaceable Christian,* 1710, in Preface.
[78] Fox, Epistle 308 (1674).
[79] *John,* 13:35.
[80] Lewis Benson, *Catholic Quakerism: a vision for all men,* Philadelphia Yearly Meeting, 1966, chapter 3.
[81] William Penn, *Works,* 1726, vol. 1, p. 842.
[82] Letter of 1653. Full text to be found in Ellwood's edition of Fox's *Journal.*
[83] Fox, *Journal,* op. cit., p. 301. Entry for 1657.
[84] *Ibid.,* p. 534. Entry for 1669.
[85] *Ibid.,* p. 180. Entry for 1654.
[86] *Ibid.,* p. 405. Entry for 1661.
[87] 'Testimonies to the Life of George Fox' in Ellwood's edition of Fox's *Journal.*
[88] Fox, *Journal,* op. cit., p. 171. Entry for 1653.
[89] Letter quoted in full in *Friends Quarterly,* April 1977 (Tuke Papers No. 81 in Barthwick Institute, York).
[90] Fox, *Journal,* op. cit., p. 199. Entry for 1655.
[91] Quoted in *The Personality of George Fox* by A. Neave Brayshaw, Allenson, 1933, p. 114.
[92] Fox, *Gospel Truth Demonstrated,* p. 742.
[93] Quoted in Brayshaw, op. cit., p. 131.
[94] Quoted in *Christion Faith and Practice,* op. cit., § 401.
[95] Bede Griffiths, *Return to the Centre,* Collins, 1976, p. 145.
[96] Harry Williams, *Becoming What I am,* Darton Longman & Todd, 1977, p. 75.
[97] Hans Küng, *On Being a Christian,* Collins, 1977, p. 278.
[98] John A. T. Robinson, *Liturgy Coming to Life,* Mowbray, 1963, p. 31.
[99] Tillich, *The Shaking of the Foundations,* op. cit., p. 120.
[100] Anthony Bloom, *School for Prayer,* Libra, 1970, p. 62.
[101] Fox, *Journal,* op. cit., p. 293. Entry for 1657.

A NOTE ON SOURCES
and
SUGGESTIONS FOR FURTHER READING

For a long time, most of Fox's writings have been hard to come by; much of his writing has never been printed, and his epistles and doctrinal books have not been issued in full since 1830. The three massive volumes printed at the turn of the seventeenth century may be read in the Libraries at Friends House, London, and Woodbrooke College, Selly Oak, Birmingham. *Gospel Truth Demonstrated* has 1,096 pages, measures 14 ins. by 9 ins. by 3½ ins., and weighs 9½ pounds! Some of the unpublished writings, giving a rather different picture from the printed material, have been transcribed by Hugh Ross, who has generously allowed me to include some extracts; it is to be hoped that much more of this will be published.

But this position is changing. Much of Fox's most profound writing is found in his collected *Epistles,* and a selection made by Cecil Sharman has recently been published by Quaker Home Service (*No More but my Love: letters of George Fox,* 1980). A full modern edition is being prepared in the United States. Fox's *Journal* has often been printed; the version most often to be found in libraries and second-hand bookshops is a full or abridged reprint of Thomas Ellwood's edition, published soon after Fox's death. But John Nickall's 1952 edition, republished by the Society of Friends in 1975, presents Fox's story in his unvarnished words and style, from manuscripts taken from his dictation. Unless otherwise stated, this is the version used in this book, by permission of the publishers, with page references and date of the year referred to.

The background to Fox's mission is explored in Christopher Hill's *The World Turned Upside Down* (Penguin, 1975). The classic study of the origins of the Society of Friends, William C. Braithwaite's *The Beginnings of Quakerism* and *The Second Period of Quakerism* (2nd edn., 1955–61, revised by Henry Cadbury, rptd. 1970 by Wm. Sessions) is wide-ranging, dispassionate, stimulating and very readable. A very helpful book, out of print but not hard to find, is A. Neave Brayshaw's *The Personality of George Fox* (Allenson, 1933). Also out of print, but available in many libraries, is Vernon Noble's straightforward historical biography of Fox, *The Man in Leather Breeches* (Elek, 1953).

I must here acknowledge my own debt to these books in particular, and to the help, suggestions and criticisms of Heather Bailey, Maurice Creasey, George Gorman, Ormerod Greenwood, Diana Lampen, Vernon Noble, Arthur Peacock, and especially Joseph Pickvance, Gerald Richards and Hugh Ross. I am deeply grateful too for my conversations with Lewis Benson, though he may not agree with everything I have written!

Readers interested in the continuity and development of Quaker thought from the seventeenth century to the present day will find a fine collection of individual and collective statements in *Christian Faith and Practice in the Experience of the Society of Friends* (Society of Friends, 1960). Apart from a few key passages, I have avoided repeating quotations by Fox and others included in it. There are several surveys of the Society today; one of the most readable and easily obtained is *Quaker by Convincement* by Geoffrey Hubbard (Penguin, 1974).

The titles of *Gospel Truth Demonstrated* and William Penn's *Primitive Christianity Revived* were chosen carefully. The essential 'further reading' for the student of these writings is to be found in the New Testament. Time and again he or she is likely to see passages of the gospels in a new and vivid light, and to assent to Fox's claim: 'I was in the Spirit in which they were given forth, and what the Lord opened in me I afterwards found was agreeable to them.'

JOHN LAMPEN